The BBC Book of

ROYAL MEMORIES

The BBC Book of
ROYAL
MEMORIES

Edited by
CAROLINE ELLIOT

BBC BOOKS

Published by BBC Books,
a division of BBC Enterprises Limited,
Woodlands, 80 Wood Lane, London W12 0TT

First published 1991

© Caroline Elliot and the Contributors 1991

ISBN 0 563 36008 9

Designed by Bill Mason

Set in Garamond by Butler & Tanner Ltd, Frome and London
Printed and bound in Great Britain by Butler & Tanner Ltd, Frome and London
Colour separations by Technik Ltd, Berkhamsted
Jacket printed by Belmont Press Ltd, Northampton

CONTENTS

LIST OF CONTRIBUTORS

RONALD ALLISON, CVO, was educated at Weymouth Grammar School, and after five years as a journalist at the *Hampshire Chronicle*, he became a reporter at the BBC in 1957. He was made Court Correspondent for BBC Television in 1969, and then in 1973 was invited to become Press Secretary to Her Majesty the Queen. When he left the Buckingham Palace Press Office in 1978 he joined Thames Television as their Controller of Sport and Outside Broadcasts and then worked there as Director of Corporate Affairs. He has written two books about the Royal Family, *The Queen* (1973) and *Charles, Prince of our Time* (1978).

PETER DIMMOCK, CVO, OBE, was an RAF Pilot Instructor and an Air Ministry Staff Officer during the Second World War. He joined the BBC in 1946 as a Television Outside Broadcasts producer and commentator, working on programmes ranging from documentaries to sporting, theatrical and public events. He was associated with many of the great ceremonial occasions, including the funeral of King George VI, the Coronation of Her Majesty The Queen, the first State Opening of Parliament covered by television, and the wedding of Her Royal Highness The Princess Margaret to Mr Antony Armstrong-Jones. He was responsible for liaison between the BBC and the Royal Family from 1963 to 1977.

TOM FLEMING, OBE, first broadcast for the BBC in 1944, and since then has made over 2000 broadcasts with 300 commentaries at royal events. These have included the Coronation in 1953, the wedding of Their Royal Highnesses The Prince and Princess of Wales, state visits to the USA and Japan, the Silver Jubilee, the Ninetieth Birthday Tribute to Her Majesty Queen Elizabeth The Queen Mother, the Trooping the Colour ceremonies from 1969 to 1988, and the funeral of the Duke of Windsor.

Also a distinguished actor and theatre director, he was co-founder of the Edinburgh Gateway Company and Founder/Director of the Royal Lyceum Company. He was Director of the Scottish Theatre Company from 1982 to 1987 and a member of the Royal Shakespeare Company from 1962 to 1964. His films include *King Lear, Mary Queen of Scots* and *With Remarkable Men*. He has also appeared in countless television plays and in the title roles of *Jesus of Nazareth* (1956), *Henry IV* Parts I and II (1960), *Weir of Hermiston* (1971) and *Reith* (1983).

FRANK GILLARD, CBE, joined the BBC as Talks Producer in 1941 but was soon moved to the News Department as a War Correspondent and saw many battles from the front line. He had a distinguished career in the BBC, becoming Head of West Regional Programmes, and after several other appointments became Managing Director of BBC Radio in 1969. He has now retired but is still heard on many different television and radio programmes as a presenter and as a contributor.

HELEN HOLMES is a qualified historian and specialises in researching royal, military and ecclesiastical events for BBC Television. She first worked for the BBC Outside Broadcasts Department in 1966 when she was asked to prepare a pamphlet on British stadiums, teams and towns for the World Cup. It was during this time that she met Senior Outside Broadcasts Producer, Antony

Craxton, who encouraged her to extend her work to cover royal events. The first big event with which she was involved was the Investiture of His Royal Highness The Prince of Wales, and now she has produced the research notes for commentators on over 150 occasions. She has also written and researched documentary programmes in this field.

ROBERT HUDSON was educated at Shrewsbury and the University of London, and during the Second World War was a Major in the Royal Artillery. From 1946 he worked as a freelance broadcaster for the BBC, then in 1954 he joined the staff as Senior Outside Broadcasts Producer in the North Region, Manchester. Three years later he became Head of Administration, North Region, followed by several years as a staff commentator. He presented several programmes, including *Today*, in the 1960s as well as commentating on sporting events (mainly cricket and rugby) and state occasions. He was a commentator at the state funeral of Sir Winston Churchill, at many of the Remembrance Day services at the Cenotaph, at twenty-one Trooping the Colour ceremonies and at many royal weddings, including that of Their Royal Highnesses The Prince and Princess of Wales in 1981. In 1969 he was appointed Head of Outside Broadcasts, Radio and he retired from the BBC in 1975 to become a freelance broadcaster and lecturer.

CLIFF MORGAN, CVO, OBE, was Head of Outside Broadcasts Group, BBC Television, between 1975 and 1987. He started working at the BBC in 1958 after a distinguished career on the rugby field playing for Wales. He worked on current affairs and sports programmes as a broadcaster, producer and editor, for both BBC and Independent Television. From 1966 to 1972 he was a freelance writer, until he was appointed Editor of BBC Radio Sport. He then moved on to become Head of Outside Broadcasts Department in

Radio and later to the same position in BBC Television where he took over the responsibility of liaison with Buckingham Palace from Peter Dimmock. Cliff Morgan is now a freelance broadcaster and writer.

JOHN OSMAN has now left the BBC and lives in France, but is a former Diplomatic and Court and Commonwealth Correspondent for BBC Radio News. He left the *Daily Telegraph* to join the BBC in 1965 as Commonwealth Correspondent and spent the next few years travelling the world as BBC Radio's Number Two Washington Correspondent (1969–72), Southern Africa Correspondent (1972–75) and Moscow Correspondent (1980–82); then in 1983 he was appointed Diplomatic and Court Correspondent. John Osman worked for forty-two years as a reporter and visited over a hundred countries.

JOHN SNAGGE, OBE, joined the BBC in 1924 as Assistant Station Director in Stoke-on-Trent. He became an announcer in 1928, working at Savoy Hill, and was later Presentation Director from 1939 to 1945, making many memorable wartime broadcasts. After the war he became Head of Presentation for the Home Service and Head of Presentation (Sound) in 1957. His voice is unforgettable and many will remember his Boat Race commentaries, as he covered that event each year from 1931 to 1980.

THE EARL OF SNOWDON, GCVO, RDI, FCSD, was educated at Eton and Jesus College, Cambridge. He is a distinguished photographer, film director and author. He has been an artistic adviser to *The Sunday Times* and Sunday Times Publications Ltd since 1962 and Constable of Caernarfon Castle since 1963. He is an Honorary Fellow of the Institute of British Photographers, the Royal Photographic Society and Manchester College of Art and Design. His television films include *Don't Count the Candles* (1968) for which he won two Hollywood Emmy Awards, St George Prize, Venice and awards at the Prague and Barcelona film festivals; *Born to be Small* (1971) which won the Chicago Hugo Award and *Peter, Tina and Steve* (1977). He presented *Snowdon on Camera* for the BBC. He has published several books including *A View of Venice, Assignments, Personal View, Israel – A First View* and *Stills 1983–87.*

GODFREY TALBOT, LVO, OBE, was a Senior News Reporter and a commentator on the staff of the BBC from 1946 to 1969 but joined the BBC several years before that in 1937. He had a distinguished career as a War Correspondent overseas where he filed reports from the front line during the Second World War and received his OBE in 1946 for his despatches. After the war he was the first person to be officially accredited to Buckingham Palace as Court Correspondent and for twenty years he travelled all round the world with various members of the Royal Family. He has written several books about the Royal Family and now spends his time as a broadcaster, lecturer and journalist.

ALUN WILLIAMS, OBE, started his career in radio as a singer and actor before the Second World War. During the war he served as a seaman in the Royal Navy and later as an Intelligence Officer in the Far East. He joined the BBC in Cardiff in 1946 and has worked as a producer and commentator ever since. He commentates in English and Welsh and has worked on several of the major royal events and state occasions, including the Investiture of His Royal Highness The Prince of Wales and the wedding of Their Royal Highnesses The Prince and Princess of Wales.

INTRODUCTION TO THE BBC BOOK OF ROYAL MEMORIES

CLIFF MORGAN, CVO, OBE

O N 6 MAY 1935 – and I have a commemorative mug to prove it – there was a street party in our village. I remember long tables across the road, Corona 'pop' and ice cream and jelly, and busy mothers in their Sunday best. There were fathers trying to sort out the three-legged races, my uncle Arthur playing the piano on the pavement and all of us were singing songs we sang in Sunday school. There were coloured balloons, flags and bunting there were no buses that day. As in every other village and town in the country, it was a holiday and all the people, despite the threat of war in Europe, were celebrating the Silver Jubilee of King George V and Queen Mary. I was just five. I still have a faded photograph of myself dressed in a sailor suit and holding my cousin Betty's hand. There may well have been radio broadcasts that day but I cannot remember.

Forty-one years later, a few weeks after the Olympic Games of 1976 in Montreal, I walked, for the first time, through the Privy Purse Door at Buckingham Palace to take part in discussions on the proposed television and radio coverage of the Silver Jubilee of Her Majesty Queen Elizabeth II. It was one of my first duties as the BBC's Royal Liaison Officer – a job inherited from my predecessor in Outside Broadcasts in BBC Television.

The Queen's Press Secretary, Ronald Allison, was a long-time friend at the BBC and he understood my tentativeness so he started talking about the events at the recent Olympic Games. The wonder of a tiny fourteen-year-old gymnast, Nadia Comaneci, from Romania who had been awarded the first ever maximum score in Olympic history; of David Wilkie's gold medal and his record-breaking swim in the 200 metres breaststroke, Britain's first men's swimming gold medal for nearly seventy years. The things I knew about were a prelude to the things I did not. Decisions were eventually made about the details of the Silver Jubilee. I found that at the meeting there were no vague, unkept promises from the members of the household staff – simply a 'yes' or a 'no'. You knew exactly where you stood and that made life simple and enjoyable.

It was also my good fortune that Sir Philip Moore – now Lord Moore – was shortly to become Private Secretary to The Queen. As P.B.C. Moore, of Blackheath and England, he had been the captain of the Barbarian rugby team when I played my first game for the club at Bedford in 1951. His advice at that time and during the many years of liaison between the Palace and the BBC, saved me from stumbling down too many wrong roads.

The Royal Liaison Office at BBC Television was initially set up to be a focal point for every request that came from the many production areas at the Corporation – a sort of clearing-house. It seemed sensible that the small and busy Press Offices at Buckingham Palace, Clarence House and the Lord Chamberlain's Office should be dealt with from one source, rather than dozens of requests arriving from the many different areas of the BBC.

On average, there are four requests a day, each very different and each to be handled in a different way. For instance, the Bulgarian Service at Bush House would like to interview the Keeper of the Royal Philatelic Collection; BBC Bristol would like to film the royal collection at Buckingham Palace; would the Prince of Wales consider reading his own story, *The Old Man of Lochnagar*?; would Princess Anne – as she was then – consider opening a new local radio station?; Television Sports Department would like to invite His Royal Highness The Duke of Edinburgh to present the Sports Personality of the Year Awards; BBC Drama would like permission to film a few sequences of a new drama at Hampton Court ... Requests like these are discussed by the staff at Buckingham Palace and, knowing that a similar list would also arrive from Independent Television, it is surprising the number of times that the answer is 'Yes', when you consider the amount of official duties that have to be undertaken by the Royal Family.

'As the births of living creatures at first are ill-shapen', says Bacon, 'so are all innovations which are the births of time'. So it was at the BBC sixty years ago; but following the early, tentative footsteps it spread its wings, and radio broadcasting breathed and stirred. It was, beyond all reasonable doubt, the advent of live outside broadcasts and, with it, engineering triumphs and commentators who painted word pictures, that fulfilled the BBC's fundamental obligation to the listeners of Britain. Suddenly men and women at their most private in their homes were transported, as if by magic carpet, to events that they would never attend themselves. Royal events were a natural for the broadcaster; at its zenith, radio reported every royal tour overseas and each day there was news of the Royal Family from the far-flung corners of the Empire.

Television came into its own and brought a new and brilliant dimension to the ceremony and colour of a royal event with coverage of the Coronation of Queen Elizabeth II at Westminster Abbey in 1953. This was a sensation and millions of viewers sat for hours around the television set to see The Queen being crowned.

On the following pages, many people who have been closely associated with broadcasting royal pageantry have written personal memories of their experiences. These are stories of ingenuity and enthusiasm and of the ever growing skill of broadcasting people who march, for most of the time, in the vanguard of society. This book is also about the privilege of mapping and signposting, making pictures and selecting words to do justice to scenes of great joy or deep sorrow.

On 29 July 1981, an estimated 750 million people around the world switched on their television sets to watch the wedding of the Prince of Wales and Lady Diana Spencer. Millions more listened to the BBC and the World Service as it relayed the joy in the streets of London and the marriage vows inside St Paul's Cathedral. This was the biggest and most spectacular outside broadcast in the long history of the BBC. For many months after that Royal wedding, letters kept arriving at the BBC expressing delight at having been able to share a momentous day of pomp and ceremony;

'My family were enjoying a swim but were never too far away from our boat in case we missed one word on our radio. We felt we were in London but in actual fact we were swimming in the Indian Ocean at the time.'

'I was in my home in Singapore, listening to the radio with my 'hankie' in my hand, and when your commentators said that the members of the Royal Family were waving to them as they passed by in their carriages, I really felt they were waving at me.'

All on a long, royal, summer's day.

THE FIRST POST-WAR ROYAL TOUR

FRANK GILLARD, CBE

Frank Gillard was a War Correspondent during the Second World War with many assignments on the front line, so his voice was well known to the public when he was asked to be in charge of the BBC's coverage of the royal tour to southern Africa in 1947. The tour lasted from January to May and was greeted with great enthusiasm. The radio reports sent back to Britain by Frank Gillard and his team evoked pictures of a different way of life, for they were experiencing a hot and busy schedule. It was welcome listening for those in Britain who were shivering their way through an extremely cold winter.

EXCEPT FOR KING GEORGE VI, who during the conflict had visited his armies in north Africa and north-west Europe, the Royal Family had been cooped up in Britain throughout the Second World War. Indeed, Princess Elizabeth and Princess Margaret had never been abroad at all. But as soon as the war was over, 'the Royals' began to think again about Empire visits, and in 1946 it was announced that early in 1947 The King and Queen, with their two daughters, would undertake a lengthy tour of South Africa, the neighbouring High Commission territories, and the two Rhodesias.

The BBC believed that there would be a considerable degree of public interest in this royal expedition, and that reports of it would bring a touch of colour and pleasure to the drab circumstances of postwar life in Britain. Moreover, informal checks with the Government and with Buckingham Palace indicated that the highest circles would favour extensive broadcast coverage. So plans were made for a reporting operation on a scale which, for the BBC of those days, was decidedly lavish.

Three well-equipped disc-recording cars were shipped out at once to South Africa, and three ex-War Correspondents, Wynford Vaughan-Thomas, Robert Dunnett and myself, were assigned to the tour. No doubt we were chosen because we were all used to improvised broadcasting in unforeseeable circumstances. I was to be the team leader. The number two man in the BBC hierarchy, Mr Basil Nicolls (later Sir Basil), took me out to lunch at a modest restaurant near Broadcasting House and, in between constant expostulation at the outrageous price (as he saw it) of every item on the menu, lectured me about my role. He had dedicated himself over the years, he said, to building up a decent relationship of confidence between 'the Royals' and the BBC. He viewed with much apprehension the necessity of handing over that responsibility to me, even for the relatively brief period of this forthcoming tour. If I did anything in South Africa to upset Their Majesties, or the royal entourage, my name would for evermore be mud in the BBC. I had better keep that in mind.

The plan was that I was to work as close as I could to the Royal Family all the time, and send back daily reports for the broadcast news bulletins. Vaughan-Thomas and Dunnett were to roam ahead of the royal route as outriders, keeping three or four days ahead of the main party, recording the colourful background of the South African scene and providing sound pictures, interviews and flashes of actuality. Their recordings would be flown to London, and married to the on-the-day reports which I would be providing by radio link, so as to build up and illustrate a full chronicle of the tour. Thus we would provide for BBC listeners a first-hand account of how South Africans were seeing 'the Royals', along with a sound picture of the South Africa which 'the Royals' themselves were seeing. It had to be a sustained operation, for while royal tours nowadays seem to be over not long after they have started, in 1947 we were to be away from Britain from late January to mid-May.

In those early post-war years there was no royal yacht. Instead Britain's newest battleship, HMS *Vanguard*, fresh from the shipyard, was commissioned and brought into service, with a ship's company of 1900, and placed at His Majesty's disposal. I was allotted a cabin in *Vanguard*, while Vaughan-Thomas and Dunnett flew out to Cape Town in an aircraft of the King's Flight.

A small room adjoining the bridge recording room of HMS *Vanguard* was made available to the BBC, and our engineers converted it into a broadcasting studio. In addition, microphone points were wired in at strategic positions in other parts of the battleship. One of these was in the Admiral's Lookout, a platform high up in the seventy-foot superstructure of *Vanguard*, and it was from there that I described the departure scene as we slowly drew away from the snow-covered Farewell Jetty at Portsmouth.

It was dawn on the bitterly cold morning of 31 January 1947, and this was the start of our 6000-mile voyage. The BBC cable carrying my words was the last link between the battleship and the dockside. Steadily it was drawn up out of the water as the ship pulled out. Then it stiffened and stretched, and finally snapped, cutting me off dramatically in mid-sentence.

But a minute before that I had almost cut myself off, for a different reason. I had heard a rustle and a whisper behind me, as I was speaking. Glancing back over my shoulder I found Her Majesty The Queen, with the two Princesses, right behind me on the narrow platform, taking a close interest in the proceedings. It was not an easy situation for a commentator to take in his stride, but I managed to stifle a gasp and carry on.

In a way, that incident right at the start set the tone for the entire tour. The Royal Family, I found, was keenly interested in broadcasting. I was surprised that they were so knowledgeable about BBC programmes. Even after all these years, I remember The Queen saying to me one day, of the famous variety show ITMA, 'The King gets so cross if we have to have people in for dinner on a Thursday evening and he has to miss the programme.' In *Vanguard* they listened, in their quarters, to most of the broadcasts from the ship, and the two Princesses were interested enough to come several times to see the little studio in action.

The public's demand for news from *Vanguard* was very strong. I was called on for eight broadcasts in the first twenty hours. The ship's radio transmitters carried my regular news reports back to London, plus a varied stream of general programmes – a ship's concert, quiz and game shows, a 'Sunday Half-Hour', interviews with interesting personalities in the ship's company, including a complete 'In Vanguard Tonight', and special items for schools, for *Children's Hour*, for *Woman's Hour* and for different BBC regions. Through the radio, millions of people seemed keen to accompany us in their imagination on this tour.

The broadcasts went out on the Home and Overseas Services of the BBC, with special material for listeners to the African Service. The feedback reports relayed to us spoke of listeners in South Africa keeping their radio sets tuned to the BBC all day long as *Vanguard* approached their shores. Some enterprising people discovered the frequencies used by *Vanguard*'s own transmitters and listened direct to the ship. They were then able to hear in advance all the material I was sending to London, and also to eavesdrop on the conversations between me and my editors – not all of which were suitable for general consumption.

As we neared the Equator, preparations were going ahead for the 'Crossing the Line' ceremonies. There was much conjecture among the ship's company about the two Princesses, and whether they would be given the traditional ducking. I soon realised that I would not be excused myself, even though I had previously crossed the Equator by air. That, it was alleged, would be regarded by Neptune as a serious

The two Princesses were excused the traditional ducking as HMS Vanguard *crossed the Equator, instead they were given an almost suffocating powdering of their faces.*

offence, warranting a double dipping. On the eve of the event, The King asked me if the BBC was going to broadcast the proceedings. My reply was that I certainly hoped to record them if I were given the chance. 'I simply must listen to it,' said The King. 'Here is the Crossing the Line ceremony, and this is Frank Gillard gargling it!'

The next morning, while the two Princesses were excused the ducking and given instead a token but almost suffocating powdering of their faces, The King himself called out my name to Neptune and I received the full treatment – as the recording still in the BBC's archives confirms. Gargling was an extremely mild word for it.

The first few days in South Africa were real killers. The intense heat of the Cape was exhausting in itself, particularly to visitors coming direct from a bitterly cold British winter. The Royals proceeded, almost non-stop, from function to function in Cape Town and its immediate neighbourhood, sometimes together, sometimes separately. Crowds everywhere were wildly excited. We needed to give the BBC's audiences the fullest possible reflection of South Africa's delirious welcome. Fortunately, the South African Broadcasting Corporation, SABC, gave us maximum support, and we were able to share their technical facilities at every point in Cape Town and also throughout the whole tour.

The climax of arrival day was the grand state banquet in the City Hall. The King was to respond to the royal toast, and his speech was to be relayed live by the BBC. It was timed for 10.00 p.m. local time, which was 8.00 p.m. in London. The immensely popular variety show *Monday Night at Eight* was cancelled for this one week to make way for the royal broadcast on the Home Service.

But South Africa was unused to state banquets, and nobody bothered much about the time. By 10.00 p.m. the meal was far from over. Wynford Vaughan-Thomas, who was to broadcast a two-minute scene-setting introduction, had to continue at great length, while I rushed around the place doing everything I could to get things speeded up. It was 10.50 when at last the Prime Minister, Field Marshal Smuts, rose to propose the toast. Even then there was a long interval, while The King smoked a cigarette, before he rose to reply. So, back in

HMS Vanguard *approaches Duncan Dock, Cape Town – Table Mountain is in the background – at the start of the royal tour of South Africa in 1947.*

Britain, this broadcast caused probably the longest over-run in the BBC's history and wrecked the entire evening's programme schedules. My chiefs in London were definitely not pleased.

From Cape Town, the Royal Family boarded the royal train to travel the length and breadth of the four provinces of the Union. That train was preceded everywhere by the pilot train, which carried the organising officials and a press contingent of massive dimensions. The pilot train was to be our home for many weeks. In it, the BBC was allotted one small compartment for living and sleeping quarters, which I shared with George Rottner, who was making BBC history as the first television cameraman to cover a royal tour. The BBC Television

Service was then in its infancy, serving only the London area. George was equipped with a massive and heavy 35 mm film camera. His was a silent film operation; when his editors wanted on-the-spot sound to go with the film, they had to do the best they could with the recorded reports which I was sending back to my masters in BBC Radio.

George's equipment alone was bulky enough to fill our small compartment to overflowing. I, too, had luggage problems, because I needed a substantial wardrobe for my role, extending all the way from top hat and frock coat, or white tie and tails, down to lounge suits and informal clothes suitable for every kind of occasion and temperature. Somehow we got our problems sorted out, desperately cramped as we were, and in fact George and I got on together remarkably well all the way.

So the royal progress proceeded, to great acclaim everywhere. Almost every day, a different city or town would enjoy its hours of glory and think itself the centre of the Empire. Smaller townships would get fleeting visits of an hour or so. The pattern of events was always the same. Local grandees were presented at the railway station. Then the royal party drove slowly around the town in open cars. The exuberant street decorations always included triumphal arches, and we soon realised that the Government had organised a pool of them, and was leap-frogging them ahead of us from place to place. Old, well recognised specimens kept cropping up again and again in towns hundreds of miles apart. The proceedings always ended at the town hall, with window or balcony appearances to wild cheering and the singing of national anthems. Few places could provide a band to lead the singing. Usually it was just a battered piano, and once there was nothing else available but a solo saxophone.

Where these little places were only a hundred miles or so apart, visits to two or three of them would be packed in between dawn and dusk. Then there were the small clusters of eager South Africans gathered by the railway track in remote places. For them the train would make an unscheduled stop of perhaps ten minutes, and 'the Royals' would dismount to shake a few more hands. They went down gold mines, inspected diamond mines, visited ostrich farms, snake parks,

The Royal Family went down gold mines and visited nature reserves, industrial installations and remote stations. Frank Gillard and the BBC team followed them everywhere collecting reports to send back to Britain.

Queen Elizabeth and the two Princesses at a garden party held in their honour by Durban City Council.

nature reserves, military and industrial installations, remote trading stations. They looked in on schools, colleges, universities. They presided at gigantic native indabas where deafening tribal rituals were performed by as many as 100 000 or more ecstatic and perspiring Africans. Every aspect of South African life was on display, and all of it was reported and described over the BBC. We were aware that we were looking at a nation which was showing the best possible face to the world, and in our reporting we tried to get behind that face, to probe and reflect the complex problems of outlook, race, colour, politics, culture and language which confronted South African society.

As we approached Pretoria, the twin capital of South Africa, a considerable crisis hit me. The Government was planning another state banquet, like the earlier one at Cape Town. Sir Alan Lascelles, the King's Private Secretary, asked me to look in on him and told me that the King would again be making a speech, and that he wished the BBC to broadcast it at home. There was a good reason for this. Britain was by now in the grip of the most severe winter of the century, and there was much hardship at home. Food was severely rationed, fuel supplies had almost run out, factories were forced to suspend operations, public transport was greatly curtailed and the public services were reduced to a minimum. Voices were being raised with the suggestion that the Royal Family should cut short the South African tour and return to share in the general misery.

The King intended to use his Pretoria speech to sympathise with people at home in Britain, but to remind them that he was also King of South Africa, and that he felt a duty to go through with a tour which had been so carefully prepared, unless circumstances at home became really desperate. It was in the best interests of the Empire that the tour should continue.

I could see the point of The King's request easily enough. But I also knew that any possibility of a repeat of the fiasco at the Cape Town banquet would be resolutely rejected by the BBC in London. I explained the BBC's point of view to Sir Alan Lascelles, adding that it would only make things a hundred times worse on a Saturday evening (for that was when it was planned) if BBC listeners had to forego some we were running into trouble. So the head waiter was summoned, and one whole course of the dinner was cancelled, on The King's order. The guests must have wondered what on earth was happening.

When London switched over to Pretoria, we were very nearly ready for the royal toast. There was just time for Wynford Vaughan-Thomas, concealed behind a bank of chrysanthemums, to describe the scene. Then I gave a signal to the Prime Minister, Field Marshal Smuts, and he rose and elegantly said his piece. The toast was drunk with great acclamation, and The King immediately began to rise to reply.

That was where it went wrong, for His Majesty was hardly on his feet before the doors all around the hall were flung open, and in marched a small army of waiters bearing decanters on their trays to refill the wine glasses. Totally disconcerted, The King sank back on to his seat, looking around at me in despair. Smuts leaned over to him and anxiously said, 'Your Majesty, the Empire is waiting', to which The King replied, 'Then I am afraid it will damn well have to wait.' Alas, I had instructed the SABC (South African Broadcasting Corporation) engineers that as The King would immediately follow the Prime Minister, they should keep the high table microphones faded up all the time. So all of South Africa heard the little exchange between Prime Minister and King, but a fortuitous crackle on the beam circuit to London mercifully blotted it from the ears of the British audience. But everyone heard The King's next sentence, 'How can I possibly go ahead until these waiters have gone?' How, indeed?

Meanwhile I signalled Wynford, who promptly seized his microphone again and proceeded with great aplomb to fill this unhappy interval, while I grabbed the head waiter and peremptorily requested that he get his staff back to their kitchens immediately. It probably took only a couple of minutes but it seemed like an age. But order and decorum were restored, The King remained calm and broadcast movingly, and as his script was shorter than we had expected, we ended the broadcast within our time span. Listeners outside the hall were totally unaware of the drama, and my chiefs back in London signalled that they were well pleased.

This royal tour was to have a magnificent climax, for at its very

ABOVE: *Frank Gillard – the team leader – sent back daily reports for the news bulletins – this was a very picturesque point overlooking the Victoria Falls.*

RIGHT: *Princess Elizabeth recording the historic broadcast on her twenty-first birthday at the Falls Hotel in Victoria. 'This will probably be the most important broadcast of my daughter's life,' said The King. The picture was taken by Frank Gillard.*

end Princess Elizabeth, the Heir to the Throne, was to celebrate her twenty-first birthday in Cape Town. On that evening she was to undertake a major broadcast. She would be speaking from Government House in Cape Town, and the SABC would have no difficulty in bringing her words to every listener in the Union. But it was the BBC's job to make certain that she could also be heard throughout the UK, the Empire, and the world at large, and for that we were utterly dependent on the beam radio link between Cape Town and London. Unfortunately that service had proved to be unreliable during our weeks in South Africa. Quite often broadcasts sent over the link had been almost inaudible at the London end. There was at least a one-in-three chance that on Princess Elizabeth's great day that vital link would let us down.

Up to this time, every royal broadcast had been live. The practice had become protocol. Somehow pre-recording was seen, in the words of John Reith, as 'a fraud on the listener'. Pre-recording by royalty was simply not done. I began to express my misgivings about the Cape Town-London link to the people of influence in the royal entourage, hinting that it would be safer if the Princess were to record her broadcast in advance so that we could fly high-quality discs to London, but nobody paid much attention. So I took the unusual step of typing a formal memorandum to Sir Alan Lascelles. This led to several meetings, because breaking with royal precedent could not be contemplated lightly, but in the end my request was granted.

I was invited to join the Royal Family at the famous Falls Hotel in Victoria on Sunday 13 April, a week or so before the birthday. First there was a short service (it was Low Sunday) in the hotel ballroom. After coffee, at about 10.30 a.m., four of us – The King, The Queen, Princess Elizabeth and myself – took to deck chairs on a quiet lawn at the back of the hotel and, in a tight circle, we worked on the script of the forthcoming broadcast. 'This will probably be the most important broadcast of my daughter's life,' The King said to me, 'and it is up to all of us, and especially you, to make it perfect.'

I still have no idea of who drafted that original script. It appalled me, and I was relieved to find that my views were fully shared around the circle. 'Can you imagine a young person of my daughter's age uttering such pompous platitudes?' The King said to me. Most certainly I could not. The four of us spent two hours rewriting the script, making it simple, unpretentious, sincere, genuine and, I thought, very moving. Thirty years later, when Queen Elizabeth celebrated the Silver Jubilee of her reign, she quoted from that text in her commemorative broadcast. Evidently it is still seen in the highest circles as a landmark of royal broadcasting.

I was invited to lunch, and then The King said to me, 'This is where you take over. Make sure you have a really thorough rehearsal before the Princess makes her recording.' We took a break for a couple of hours, and by then my engineering colleague, Stanley Unwin, had arrived and we set up a microphone at a small table on the hotel terrace by the lawn. Shortly before sundown, Princess Elizabeth joined us, composed, confident and extremely co-operative. The rehearsals went well and the recording was excellent. Within hours the discs were on their way to London. On 21 April, the actual birthday, the beam radio service, as it happened, was behaving well, and the broadcast came live from Government House in Cape Town, as planned. But in London the discs of the pre-recording were standing by, ready for use at a second's notice if the beam transmission deteriorated. In any case our work on the script, and the time spent in rehearsal at the Falls Hotel, paid off handsomely. The historic broadcast was hailed with approval, world-wide.

'I declare before you all that my whole life, whether it be long or short, shall be devoted to your service and the service of our great Imperial family to which we all belong. But I shall not have the strength to carry out this resolution alone unless you join in it with me as I now invite you to do. I know that your support will be unfailingly given. God help me to make good my vow and God bless all of you who are willing to share in it.'

Princess Elizabeth's words of dedication in that broadcast were, of course, spoken in the knowledge that in the normal course of events she would one day become Queen. But nobody could foresee how soon that day would come. Less than five years later she and the Duke of Edinburgh, to whom she was by then married, set out on a grand tour which was planned to take them on visits to Commonwealth countries right across the globe. Once again, I was the leader of the BBC team covering an extensive royal journey.

Kenya was our first stop. On 3 February 1953, after days of exhausting ceremonial events in Nairobi, the royal couple drove 100 miles over rough tracks to the Sagana Lodge, deep in forest country 7000 feet up in the foothills of Mount Kenya. The Lodge had been Kenya's wedding gift to them. The media have to be on hand, even on royal rest days, in case of unexpected events, so I followed the royal party and stayed at the Outspan Hotel in the nearby village of Nyeri.

Ten miles away, in the heart of the Aberdare Forest, accessible only by rough forest track and then by a winding, narrow footpath through the dense bush, was the famous Treetops Hotel. In those days it was simply a three-roomed wooden shack, built thirty-five feet above the ground in the branches of a huge Mgumu (wild fig) tree which stood at the edge of a small forest clearing and waterhole. The narrow balcony of the hotel provided a marvellous observation platform, revealing the wildlife of Africa by night as well as by day because of artificial moonlight run from accumulators.

Early on the afternoon of 5 February we watched the progress of the royal car through the brightly decorated streets of Nyeri. 'Welcome to our future Queen' read one of the home-made banners across the roadway. The next few hours were to give that greeting a poignant meaning. The car moved slowly, mile after mile, up the rough forest track until it could go no further. The Princess, in yellow bush shirt and brown slacks, then set out with her husband and a guide along the narrow footpath ahead, disappearing almost immediately from our view.

At nine o'clock the next morning, the little party reappeared. The Princess was full of stories of the wild beasts of the night – elephant, rhinoceros, waterbuck, giraffe, hyena, jackal, impala, zebra – all seen from the balcony of Treetops. It had been a memorable night of vivid excitement. 'I must get my father to come out here,' she said to me; 'he would simply love all this.' So we dispersed.

The Durbar.
"He Caliphs Armies driving their slaves before them"

Wynford Vaughan-Thomas, a member of the 1947 broadcasting team,
was a veteran of royal tours. He used to sketch
the scenes he commentated on. This one is from the
royal tour of Nigeria in 1956.

Two hours later, the unbelievable news reached us. Back in England, at Sandringham, on that same night, The King had died. Elizabeth, who had climbed up to Treetops as Princess had, unwittingly, come down again as Queen. The Duke of Edinburgh was told first, and he broke the news to his wife. 'She bore it like a Queen,' he said afterwards.

Hurried arrangements had to be made. Three hours later the royal car passed through Nyeri again. This time the streets were silent, and the decorations were down – except the Union Jacks which had been nailed to their staffs and could not be lowered. The little procession headed for Nanyuki, on the Equator, thirty-seven miles away, and of the most popular programmes of the whole week, just waiting by their radio sets until Pretoria was ready for His Majesty to speak. Speaking colloquially to Sir Alan, who was a very good friend, I said, 'Millions at home will say, "here are we in Britain cold and hungry, and there is the King in South Africa so busy guzzling that he can't even speak to us on time".' Lascelles, with a grave face, said, 'I think you had better explain this to The King yourself,' and took me to The King's cabin.

King George VI listened to me patiently, but at the end he said, 'I still want to broadcast, and if you can't arrange it I shall invoke Attlee.' Attlee, of course, was the Prime Minister, and I knew well enough that the very last thing my bosses wanted was an intervention from Downing Street. Desperately, I said to The King, 'Sir, it might be possible to arrange the broadcast if it could be guaranteed that you would be speaking at a fixed time.' The King said, 'That must be arranged; you go and see everybody involved and tell them it is a royal order.' He added, 'Start with The Queen herself, and be sure you see The Queen's dresser. She is the one who often makes us late. And see Smuts and all his people.'

Now the cables began passing rapidly between me and the BBC's planners in London. Eventually I got them to recognise that this was a 'royal command' situation and, on my solemn promise of a strictly punctual start, provision was made in the Home Service programme schedule for a relay of The King's speech from Pretoria. The King was pleased. Smuts issued instructions to all and sundry about timing the banquet precisely. The Queen was as helpful as ever, and her dresser was instructed about her responsibilities in the matter. I thought there was a good chance that my guarantee would be honoured.

On the night, it all started well. The huge attendance gathered – the aristocracy of the nation, 800 guests. 'The Royals' arrived right on time. When he reached his chair, The King looked around for me, gave me a wave, and then ostentatiously removed the watch from his wrist and placed it by his plate. But the service was alarmingly slow. I became increasingly worried, and so did His Majesty. He called me over and we checked our estimates. Smuts joined in. We agreed that arrived at the small landing strip there just as dusk was closing in. Now wearing a beige dress, with a white hat and belt, Elizabeth mounted the steps of the small, waiting aircraft and in a few moments she was away in the night to begin her new life as Queen. And I got into my ancient taxi (the best that Nyeri could offer) for the 150-mile drive over forest tracks, through the African night and its roaming wildlife, to the waiting microphone at the Cable and Wireless station back in Nairobi.

But those historic days in Kenya lay in the unknown future as, in 1947, the first great post-war royal tour, the visit to South Africa, moved to its climax.

On a glorious spring morning, 11 May, exactly 100 days since the departure from the snow-bound and almost deserted Farewell Jetty at Portsmouth, HMS *Vanguard* sailed proudly up the English Channel towards her base. It was a Sunday, and a huge, unofficial convoy assembled on those calm and sparkling waters to give the Royal Family a resounding people's welcome home. Almost everything on the south coast that could float was at sea that day – sailing craft, motor boats, power boats, pleasure craft, paddle steamers, even rowing boats, mingling cheerfully with the official naval escort. Flags and streamers were everywhere. Whistles, sirens, klaxon horns, revved-up engines, and great, incessant bursts of cheering and singing echoed loudly across the water. The Royal Family stood for a very long time on their special platform on B turret just forward of *Vanguard*'s bridge, in full view of the multitude. From the Admiral's Lookout I was on continuous duty, trying to give an impression of this huge, spontaneous, sustained demonstration to listeners at home and abroad. Here was welcome proof that Britain at large had approved of the royal tour and had followed its course with interest. Broadcasting had certainly been a main agency in building and holding that interest. The Royal Family knew that, and said as much when I was summoned to their quarters just before lunch to say goodbye. As a souvenir, they gave me a grand, autographed photograph. It is a trophy which I still greatly prize, though in truth my memories of those eventful weeks are still so vivid that I need no souvenir to rekindle them.

THE CORONATION OF HER MAJESTY QUEEN ELIZABETH II

JOHN SNAGGE, OBE

For many people, John Snagge was the voice of the Oxford and Cambridge Boat Race which he covered for radio for fifty years. However, his most momentous broadcast was from Westminster Abbey at the Coronation of Her Majesty Queen Elizabeth II on 2 June 1953. He was BBC Radio's Chief Announcer at the time and it was a great surprise to him to be asked to commentate at the Coronation as he recalls in the following interview.

I NEVER KNEW WHY I WAS CHOSEN to commentate on the service of the Coronation for the Home Service. In those days I was known as 'The Voice of the Boat Race', and I had a job in Presentation, sorting out programmes. But I distinctly remember the day they asked me to do it. I was in my office, I had my uncle with me, Uncle Arthur who was an admiral in the Navy, when the telephone rang. It was Basil Nicolls, Acting Director General. He said, 'John, we've just had a meeting with the Governors and it's been unanimously agreed that you should commentate on the Coronation from Westminster Abbey.' I said, 'What me?' I thought that they'd have a padre doing it like they did for the first broadcast Coronation in 1937.

From that moment, my life became the Coronation. I began by contacting the three people in charge: the Earl Marshal, the Duke of Norfolk, who was responsible for the ceremonials; Dr William McKie (later Sir William) who was Director of Music; and the Archbishop of Canterbury, Dr Geoffrey Fisher who was, obviously, responsible for the religious part of the ceremony.

One of the first things we did was to decide where to put the microphones in the Abbey. R. H. Wood, who was Senior Outside Broadcasts Engineer, and I stood at the altar talking to the Duke of Norfolk about where they should go. Wood, of course, wanted to put them where they would be most effective, but Norfolk was worried about them being too obvious; the microphones were very ugly and it wasn't considered the done thing for them to show, even then. Norfolk knew where the microphones had been for the Coronation of King George VI in 1937, and when Wood said he wanted a microphone on the altar, Norfolk said that the BBC didn't have one there last time, and showed Wood where they had been hidden in the arms and carved back of St Edward's Chair (the Coronation chair). As a compromise, we decided to place the microphones in faldstools, on lecterns, inside light fittings and under the arms of chairs, with cables tucked along skirting boards and under carpets. Altogether there were thirty-two microphones in the Abbey, I think.

Quite apart from all our preparations for broadcasting, the Abbey had its own preparations to make. It was closed for six months so that huge stands could be erected in the transepts and in the aisles for the peers: south for the peers and north for the peeresses. The Abbey usually holds 2000, but for the Coronation the seating capacity was quadrupled to 8000.

The preparation was intense. There were meetings and rehearsals for two months beforehand: music rehearsals, ceremonial rehearsals, rehearsals for the choir and rehearsals for the clergy. We also had two full dress-rehearsals in which the Duchess of Norfolk deputised for The Queen. One of these was filmed from beginning to end to give the technicians a chance to check their timing and their camera positions, and to give the Duke of Norfolk, Dr William McKie and the Archbishop of Canterbury a chance to see what it would look like – in colour – on television. It was one of the greatest tasks the BBC engineers had ever undertaken. The dress rehearsals also helped me to see how the different parts of the ceremony fitted together, and they gave me an idea of the timing of the whole thing. I prayed that the dress rehearsal timing would be roughly equivalent to the timing of the actual ceremony.

The day before the Coronation I walked beside the Duke of Norfolk humming the National Anthem so that he could set the pace from the altar to the organ screen exactly in time with the Anthem. I hummed the Anthem at the pace at which I assumed it would be played. The first time we did it, he said, 'That won't do and we must do it again.' So we did it again. Whether he paid any attention to my humming I don't know, but it was a curious thing to be asked to do when the timing of the service had nothing to do with me at all.

The rehearsals gave me confidence in so far as the practicalities of the ceremony were concerned, but I was very worried about what I was going to do if something went wrong. It was always possible, for example, that The Queen would faint. The heat from the television lights was terrific and she wore such enormously heavy robes most of the time. The crown alone weighed nearly five pounds. The peers and peeresses, some of whom were quite elderly, also wore tremendously heavy robes and coronets; and the length of the service in itself, without the added heat of the televison lights, was enough to make anyone pass out. Norfolk, poor chap, was suffering from appalling gout. He described it to me afterwards as very 'discomfortable'.

It was perfectly possible that something would happen unexpectedly: one of the attendants carrying one of the swords of state might have fallen on his face – anything could have happened. It was my permanent worry because what on earth was I going to say if something went wrong. I couldn't ignore it, because it would be in the press the next day and everyone would know about it and say, 'Well, why didn't you mention it?' But what would I say?

As it happened, nothing very serious did go wrong, although I remember one amusing anecdote. There was a moment when I couldn't actually see the altar, but I saw the Archbishop move to the altar and I'd just said, 'The Archbishop moves to the altar to announce the Introit "O God our Defender",' and I sat back with the headphones on waiting for him to say the Introit. To my astonishment a voice said, 'Let us pray.' Well that wasn't on my script at all! I thought, 'I'm in the wrong place at the wrong time at the wrong ceremony and I've got the wrong script in front of me.' There was quite a pause and then finally the Archbishop went back and said, ' "O God Our Defender", the Introit,' – that was quite a relief.

Three or four days later I had to go down to Lambeth Palace to see the Archbishop about another broadcast and we obviously talked about the Coronation service. 'Did anything go wrong as far as you were concerned?' he asked. 'I gather all went well.' And I said, 'Yes sir, it did'. He said, 'Did nothing go wrong at all?' and I said, 'No sir, not really.' 'What about the Introit?' he asked, to which I replied, 'Well, yes, that was an ugly moment.' He explained that he had turned over two pages at once but that the chaplain quickly put him right. 'It must have been awkward for you. What did you do during the pause? Did you say anything?' And I said, 'No, sir, I didn't. But I did exactly what you told me to do if anything did go wrong: I prayed. And there was nobody in the Abbey praying harder than me at that moment.'

The place where I broadcast from, a small commentary box in the triforium, was about six feet high and about three feet six inches wide. It was soundproofed so that our broadcasting could not be heard in the Abbey, but this meant that it was also unventilated. Howard Marshall, one of the BBC's best known pre-War commentators, who delivered the radio commentary on George VI's Coronation in 1937, was a very large man, and he and I had to stay side by side in this tiny unventilated box for hours sitting on a hard wooden seat, watching the ceremony through our glasses. It was very cramped indeed; we were packed in like a couple of sardines. Occasionally we did come out for a breather, but I couldn't take a break for long because I had to watch the service in case something unexpected happened.

The other commentators, who were in the annexe by the west door at the opposite end of the Abbey from us, were Audrey Russell

John Snagge in the commentary box at Westminster Abbey. After the broadcast he received a personal, handwritten note from the Archbishop of Canterbury which said, 'My Dear Snagge, may I say that from everyone I have heard how perfectly you did your part – never intruding, saying just what was needed to help the listeners to enter fully into the service.'

for the BBC and Captain (Ted) Briggs for the Canadian Broadcasting Corporation. Richard Dimbleby did the television commentary. There was an engineer outside our commentary box, but no producer.

This was the first time the Coronation ceremony had been televised, which added to the tension. I had the 1937 radio script, which was a distinct advantage in terms of the kind of language to use. The BBC considered the 1937 radio commentary a huge success at the time but we thought it was awful when we listened to it. The words I used had to be in keeping with the actual rubrics of the ceremony as they were printed in the order of service itself. I couldn't colloquialise them and I couldn't bring them into modern day language. And I also realised that when I actually spoke I had to speak at a pace which was in accordance with the movement of people. You see, no one walks at a coronation, they move, and they all moved slowly, steadily and with great dignity. It was not exactly a football commentary. In fact it wasn't a commentary at all, it was more of a guide to what was going to happen, where it was going to happen and who was going to speak. My job was to explain the order of service. Howard Marshall described the scene. I guided the listener through the ceremony. I had to be sure that I didn't find myself speaking at the same time as, for instance, the Archbishop was praying. I had to make sure that my comments fitted in with the service and with the pauses and gaps. I had to keep one eye on the service in case the Archbishop moved a bit quicker or a bit slower.

I was never really sure what might happen next, even though I had a script. And I knew I had to get it right first time; there would be no second chances. My words must not jar with what people were hearing, I was very conscious of that; and as it was a live broadcast being heard by the world, I kept thinking there are people who've got strange views and old-fashioned views and modern views, and somehow I had to do something which didn't destroy people's individual reverence for the monarchy, but which explained the service at the same time. I found it was terribly difficult to keep my eye on the proceedings and yet not to stumble, not to be uncertain, and to give the impression that I knew exactly what was going on even if I didn't.

The knowledge that the Commonwealth and the American people were probably more enthusiastic than a great many people in Britain, and that those people were listening, made me acutely aware of my duty both to the ceremony itself and to the audience. Eighty-three per cent of the British population received the transmission via the Home Service and it was broadcast to the Commonwealth, the British Forces overseas and English-speaking people throughout the world. It was, at that time, the biggest broadcasting operation of all time. All the American networks took it and television coverage went direct to France, Holland, Belgium and West Germany. I knew it was going to have a colossal audience. It was ninety-three per cent appreciation, which was terrific in those days. (The Audience Appreciation Index is a voluntary public listening panel which the BBC used, and still uses, to measure how much, or how little, a programme is liked, as distinct from the actual numbers of people who listen to a programme.)

I don't think I slept at all the night before. I stayed in Sloane Street and I arrived at the Abbey at about five o'clock in the morning. The weather was beastly, it rained most of the day. I arrived early partly because I didn't want to get caught up in any of the processions, but mostly because I wanted to settle down and have a good look at the Abbey, get my bearings, get myself settled. There was a long, long wait until the service started at eleven o'clock, but it had its practical uses: by being there before anyone else I had the advantage of seeing the people coming in and of being able to locate the VIPs as they sat down. On arrival at the Abbey all those dignitaries took their places with the minimum of fuss. Only Churchill put on a bit of an act. He was wearing his Garter robes and Lady Churchill wore the rose-pink silk mantle of the Order of the British Empire and they came up from the west door under the organ loft and he did a little act, bowing and waving his hand, because most people hadn't seen him arrive. It was, I think, a personal gesture, but he was the only person who made anything out of his own entrance.

It took three or four hours for the people to come in, and gradually the picture built up against the magnificent backdrop of blue and gold carpets and hangings. From my small box high up in the triforium of the Abbey, I looked down on the altar. I was directly above Edward the Confessor's tomb and chapel, and I could see the full length of the Abbey to the West door. Below me, where the transepts intercept, was the raised platform known as the Theatre, and in the centre of the Theatre stood the great Coronation Throne, St Edward's Chair, with the Stone of Scone below it, the stone of destiny which was placed there by Edward I and which looks, as Howard Marshall said in 1937, like 'a rough craggy slab of hard sandstone, too heavy for a man to lift'. The carpet beneath St Edward's Chair was gold, and the carpet which ran from the steps of the Theatre to the west door was blue. The old stone of the Abbey was decorated with blue and gold hangings.

Every king and queen of England since William the Conqueror, except Edward V who died so young and Edward VIII who abdicated, has been crowned at Westminster with a virtually unchanged ceremony. And on this historic day, news of another landmark was being whispered through the assembling crowds in the Abbey. Everest had been conquered on 29 May. Everest conquered, Queen Elizabeth crowned, what more could we possibly want? Richard Dimbleby wrote later that he'd never felt the strain of a public event so much, and I agree with him. But it was at some point during that long wait before the service began that I said to myself that whatever I did after this broadcast, this would still be the climax. 'There's nothing I can do after this one.'

Although our preparation was intense, the one thing the rehearsals had not prepared me for was the emotion of the ceremony. I was completely caught up in the emotion and several times I remember suddenly pulling myself together and thinking, 'Goodness what's my next cue,' because I was so moved by what was going on in front of

The Queen looked superb at the Coronation in a shimmering white satin dress designed by Norman Hartnell. The royal robe of crimson velvet, hemmed with ermine and bordered with gold lace, was carried by the maids of honour.

me. The most powerful memory of the whole service was the opening, I think – that was the moment when I was hit smartly between the eyes. The processions were magnificent and the organ music wonderful – Holst and Vaughan Williams, Elgar and Handel – but when the great moment of the entry of The Queen and her procession came, I was overwhelmed. Handel's 'Firework Music' on the organ, everyone standing, and then Parry's anthem 'I Was Glad' during which great shouts came from the Westminster School boys of, 'Vivat Regina! Vivat Regina Elizabetha! Vivat! Vivat!' It was the most moving moment.

The Queen looked superb in a shimmering white satin dress designed by Norman Hartnell. The royal robe of crimson velvet, hemmed with ermine and bordered with gold lace, was carried by the maids of honour. The Queen wore a diadem, bracelets and necklaces. The hem of her gown was embroidered with British and Commonwealth emblems. She absolutely glittered, and there was a gasp from everyone when she appeared. Hartnell said later that he had an awful time keeping the dress hidden from the Press. Their photographers were installed in the house opposite his so he had all his windows blacked out to foil them.

The service of the Coronation began with the presentation of The Queen to the congregation, the Recognition and the Oath, and ended with the procession in which she shows herself, crowned and robed, to the people. It has always been the rule that as many people as possible should be present in the Abbey and that as many more should see the procession. Television made it possible, for the first time, for almost everyone in the land to take part in the Recognition.

After the Archbishop said to the congregation, 'Sirs, I here present unto you Queen Elizabeth, your undoubted Queen, wherefore all you who are come this day to do your homage and service. Are you willing to do the same?', there were great cries of 'God Save Queen Elizabeth' from the congregation. The Queen acknowledged the cries four times and each time the thunder of voices seemed to grow in volume. In those few clamorous moments the whole atmosphere in the Abbey changed; everyone was irrevocably involved.

The second part of the service was the Annointing and the Consecration which is the purely religious and private part of the ceremony. It was performed 'in private' under a golden canopy held by four Knights of the Garter to conceal The Queen and the Archbishop from the gaze of the congregation. Just before the Annointing the whole orchestra, the organ and the massive choir broke into *Zadok the Priest*, the music specially written by Handel for King George II's Coronation and performed at every Coronation since. It was overpowering. From where I stood I could look down and just see beneath the canopy so I watched the actual annointing. I, the BBC crew and the Archbishop himself were the only people who saw that part of the ceremony; it was not televised, and the rest of the congregation could not see it. The Queen wore no jewellery at that point and she had nothing on her head. Her crimson robe was removed and she wore a simple white linen gown over her shimmering dress, as simple as it was possible to be, and I remember being terribly impressed by the sudden simplicity in the middle of the gorgeousness of it all, the dignity and loneliness of The Queen and the silence that surrounded her at that moment.

The third part of the service was the Investiture, a civil ceremony, in which the proper officers of Church and State signify that authority has been lawfully transferred from the last monarch to the successor. After the Queen was annointed, she wore several robes. The first, known as the Colobium Sidonis of pure white linen, the second, the Supertunica, a long coat of gold lined with rose-coloured silk, and the third, the Pallium, which was presented to her as part of the Investiture, and which is the Royal Robe of the Cloth of Gold. At the Investiture, the Archbishop, the Bishops and the various men of state presented The Queen with golden spurs, symbols of chivalry; the Sword of State; a pair of Armills (bracelets) which are symbols of sincerity and wisdom; the Robe of the Cloth of Gold with which the Dean of Westminster, Dr Alan Don robed her; the Orb which is placed in her right hand; The Queen's ring, often called the wedding ring of England, on the fourth finger of her right hand; a white kid glove presented by Lord Wootton, the Chancellor of the Duchy of Lancaster;

and two sceptres both presented at the same time, one into each hand, one representing justice and the other mercy, as a sign that justice and mercy should always go together.

The colours were absolutely staggering. In the north transept were, perhaps, 200 peeresses in their red and ermine robes. Then there were the green, blue and scarlet mantles of the Order of Chivalry, the full dress military and diplomatic uniforms and the exotic costumes from the far corners of the globe, the clergy in their superb embroidered copes and the Heralds in their quartered tabards. And then, oddly noticeable in all that pageantry, was the Moderator of the General Assembly of the Church of Scotland, the Right Reverend Dr J. Pitt-Watson, who stood out by sheer contrast. He wore a simple black robe and surplice, no colour anywhere. The Moderator was taking part in the Coronation ceremony for the first time: his task was to present the Bible to The Queen.

Finally the great moment of the crowning came. It was the most dramatic moment in the ceremony. However, I knew that the Archbishop was a bit troubled by the Crown. He had great difficulty getting it the right way round and so he tied a tiny piece of cotton to the front of the Crown to make sure that he would put it on correctly. At the moment The Queen was crowned, there came great shouts from all the congregation, from the peers and from the peeresses, from everybody shouting 'Her Majesty The Queen'.

It was a very moving ceremony and somehow very simple, yet performed by people wearing the most sumptuous materials, gold and jewels I have ever seen. It was like an epic film, but the difference between an epic film and what happened in Westminster Abbey was that all those people in their robes and in their regalia were real. There were no actors there, they were all people entitled to wear such robes, entitled to carry such symbols of office. All their positions had been handed down through the centuries of history attached to Britain and the Commonwealth.

When I looked down and saw this piece of history unfolding before me, this piece of history which followed in the footsteps of so many great kings and great queens, I was moved by the magnificent

Her Majesty The Queen is crowned.
The Archbishop had tied a tiny piece of cotton
to the front of the crown to make sure that
he put it on correctly.

sight. I was moved by the colour, the ceremony and the crowds, the gaudiness, the pomp and the dignity, but most of all, by the way The Queen conducted herself and by my sense of the enormous responsibility that she alone carried, and by her utter loneliness in the middle of this great crowd. It was overwhelming. The danger was that I didn't want to talk at all. It was so emotional that I just wanted to look and look and not say a word, but I had to control myself and act as a professional. I think Richard Dimbleby felt exactly the same thing. It was hard to do your duty. After all the rehearsals it should have been straightforward, but being struck by such intense emotion is not something you can rehearse or control, and nobody could help

ABOVE: *The scene outside the Abbey as the newly crowned monarch emerged. It was a wet day but it didn't deter hundreds of thousands of people from watching the processions.*

LEFT: *As The Queen left Westminster Abbey the whole place erupted into a thunder of noise of choir and orchestra.*

being struck by the emotion of the occasion. Many people were in tears, and I had to kick myself and say, 'Stop it, Snagge. Get on with your job.' There was an American Colonel who was standing behind us and he had tears streaming down his face. He kept saying, 'I don't believe it. I just don't believe it.' Even the clergy were mopping their eyes.

After the crowning, the representatives of the various grades of peers paid homage to The Queen. They knelt before her, gave the words of loyalty and then kissed her hand. The Duke of Edinburgh took the oath on behalf of all the dukes. Only once before in English history, in 1702 when Prince George of Denmark did homage to Queen Anne, had a husband done homage to his wife. The words which he said have not changed for centuries, 'I Philip, Duke of Edinburgh, do become your liege man of life and limb, and of earthly worship; and faith and truth I will bear unto you, to live and die, against all manner of folks. So help me God.' Then he stood and kissed his Queen, his wife, on her cheek. After the Duke of Edinburgh, the Dukes of Gloucester and of Kent paid homage, then the Earl Marshal, the Duke of Norfolk, and then the Marquess of Huntley, the Earl of Shrewsbury, Viscount Arbuthnot and Baron Mowbray, each representing a branch of the peerage.

The homage is not as simple as it sounds because after paying homage they had to walk backwards about seven steps, wearing those enormous robes. There was one chap who, as he came down the steps backwards holding the robe out behind him, turned to pick up his coronet which was being held by a page on a cushion. For some reason or another he threw his hands behind his back which flung his robes into the air and I could see everybody ducking back to avoid the flying robes. As I looked down I could see several people trying not to smile.

As The Queen left the Abbey, the whole place erupted into a thunder of noises from choir and orchestra. I was awfully sorry that it had ended; I could have watched it for ages. I had a terrible feeling in my bones that I'd made a mess of it somehow and so I was dreading going back to Broadcasting House. I fought my way through the mob of people – the crowds outside the Abbey were solid, you couldn't

The Queen and the Duke of Edinburgh with a young Prince Charles and Princess Anne appear on the balcony of Buckingham Palace in answer to chants of 'We want The Queen'.

get transport. I walked most of the way and I got back to Great Portland Street and thought, 'I don't dare go in. I'm going to get a roasting from the bosses. I'm sure I've made some awful mistake.' I went to the local pub and got a drink or two before braving Broadcasting House. The owner of the pub, George Evans, came up to me after a while and said, 'You're wanted on the telephone.' I went to the telephone and a voice said, 'This is Lindsay Wellington,' who was the sort of boss of programmes (Director of Sound Broadcasting). 'I've been wondering where the hell you were,' he said, 'and someone suggested the pub.'

'This is it,' I thought.

And he said, 'I just wanted to say congratulations. We all thought it was splendid. Absolutely first rate.'

'Thank God for that,' I thought. 'At least I can show my face in the place again.'

TELEVISING
THE
CORONATION

PETER DIMMOCK, CVO, OBE

The Coronation of Her Majesty Queen Elizabeth II was the biggest live event to challenge the staff working at BBC Television since the service was started. The previous Coronation service in 1937 had not been televised 'live' and even in 1953 there was opposition to having cameras inside Westminster Abbey. Peter Dimmock was the BBC producer responsible for the occasion and it took many long months of negotiation before permission was received to go ahead and cover the day from beginning to end.

WHEN I WAS INVITED TO CONTRIBUTE a chapter to this *BBC Book of Royal Memories* it had to be, for me, Coronation day 1953. Not only was I lucky enough to be the Television Outside Broadcast Producer and Director of the Coronation service from Westminster Abbey, but I was also Chief Executive to the late S. J. 'Lobby' Lotbiniere, Head of BBC Television Outside Broadcasts. We were responsible for the overall planning and execution of all the television outside broadcasts on that historic day. It must still rank as one of the most complex and, because of the near obsolescence at that time of much of the technical equipment, riskiest, of major live royal events. In fact, it subsequently marked the beginning of public recognition of the new medium of television at the expense of what was becoming affectionately known as 'steam radio'. The sale of television sets really took off.

An enormous amount of near cloak-and-dagger negotiations took place over many months before permission was finally given for the BBC to cover the Coronation service in full from Westminster Abbey with television outside broadcast cameras. At that time in the early fifties, television was still considered by the Establishment to be nothing more than an unwelcome 'peeping Tom' and its programmes were never a topic of conversation at dinner parties!

Initially there was to be no television coverage inside the Abbey. Winston Churchill, the Cabinet and a large number of eminent people were against it. It was also suggested that the Royal Family were not too keen on it either, but I never believed this to be entirely true. Our first task therefore was to make every effort to overturn the official refusal to allow the centrepiece of the day, the service from Westminster Abbey, to be televised. This we did by continuously lobbying the Government; The Queen's Private Secretary, Sir Alan Lascelles; the Earl Marshal, the Duke of Norfolk; the Archbishop of Canterbury, Dr Geoffrey Fisher; the Dean of Westminster, Dr Alan Don, and practically everyone else that we could think of who might possibly influence a change of decision!

Eventually we achieved partial success. The Government agreed that we could place television cameras in the Abbey, but only to the west of the choir screen. This meant that we were still not allowed to cover the actual service. This was patently absurd and would have infuriated viewers. It would also have caused unnecessary resentment for the Royal Family and the Government as it would have been interpreted as the wish of the Establishment to protect their privileged position. In point of fact, one of the major and realistically valid arguments in favour of the ban was the need for special and, admittedly, very bright television lighting in the Abbey. There was also still in existence the rule that no television or film newsreel camera should be

The scene in The Mall a few days before the Coronation of Her Majesty Queen Elizabeth II as BBC Television prepared for its biggest outside broadcast since the service had begun.

closer than thirty feet from Her Majesty The Queen at any time. It is very hard to imagine now what a different set of attitudes and circumstances faced the television outside broadcast producer in the fifties and early sixties.

As Coronation day came ever closer, our lobbying began to produce results. We were given permission to hold a trial in the Abbey with a television camera facing the altar, to demonstrate what any coverage of the actual ceremony would look like. For this experiment I used a wide-angle 2″ lens to make everything appear distant and as innocuous as possible. Happily, no one thought to ask to see pictures from a 6″, 8″ or 12″ lens. Both the Earl Marshal and the Archbishop

ABOVE: *The television coverage was planned like a military operation. There were several cameras along the processional route, with commentators Brian Johnston and Bernard Braden identifying the personalities.*

LEFT: *The Coronation procession moves through Trafalgar Square on the way to Westminster Abbey. The crowds had been camping out for days.*

of Canterbury, who were there to see the demonstration, seemed reasonably happy with the pictures. However, Commander Richard Colville, The Queen's Press Secretary, dampened our optimism by again expressing concern over the amount of special lighting needed for the television cameras.

After several further nail-biting days of apprehension we were suddenly given the 'all clear' by the Government. We were to be allowed to have three of our five television cameras to the east of the choir screen in the Abbey. The Coronation service would be televised live!

The planning that has to go into the television presentation of any major event is considerable – and in the case of the Coronation was prodigious. Our aim was to give the viewer at home the very best available seat for all the day's events from early morning until the final balcony scenes from Buckingham Palace and the fireworks display. Even after that we planned a reflective piece on the significance of the great occasion from the stillness of Westminster Abbey. This was brilliantly narrated by Richard Dimbleby who had been the main television commentator throughout the day.

We planned our overall television coverage of the Coronation like a military operation. While the service in the Abbey was the centrepiece we also had to cover, as continuously as possible, the procession and all the arrivals and departures at Buckingham Palace and the Abbey. First of all, therefore, we had to assess the amount of mobile equipment that we could muster. By bringing to London our mobile units from the regions and adding some equipment from the studios we were able to press into action on the day a total of twenty-one live television cameras.

Five of these cameras were used inside the Abbey and controlled from a television production hut constructed alongside the Henry VIII Chapel. There were five further cameras outside the Abbey at various

RIGHT: *Richard Dimbleby, the television commentator in the Abbey,*
wrote later that he'd never felt the strain
of a public event so much.

vantage points, one of which was high up on Abbey House so that we could also make use of it later for skyline shots of the fireworks. Another five cameras were at Buckingham Palace; three on the Victoria Memorial, one in the Palace forecourt and one on the roof covering The Mall. On the processional route, three cameras were on the embankment near the Royal Air Force memorial. Three more cameras were at Hyde Park, on Grosvenor Gate, to obtain 'head-on' shots of the procession to make it easier for the commentators, Brian Johnston and Bernard Braden, to identify the various personalities and components.

The main commentary burden fell on Richard Dimbleby who was based in the Abbey. I had enjoyed the privilege of working with him as his Outside Broadcasts Producer on events ranging from major state occasions to more humble factory visits. Richard accepted assignments on television for as little as twelve guineas in the early post-war days, when at that time he was receiving vastly higher fees for working on radio. He did this, he told me, because he had come to the conclusion that television, and not radio, would be the mass communications medium of the future. He realised that he could master the new technique – and learn from his rare mistakes – while the size of the television audience was still small. His great ability as a distinguished war correspondent, together with his splendid command of the English language, quickly established him as 'number one'. Any major television outside broadcast without Richard as commentator was unthinkable. Also, he built up a great reputation in the television studios on programmes such as *Panorama*, and on election nights.

Whenever he accepted a television outside broadcast assignment his preparatory work was impeccable. He would be sure to have a great deal more information than he was likely to need and never minded about not using it all. It did, however, mean that he was never short of material to cover unexpected delays – Princess Margaret's wedding day was a prime example. When the newly-weds didn't arrive at the Pool of London on schedule to join the royal yacht, *Britannia*, Richard was able to tell viewers more about the Tower of London and the surrounding riverside than I believe the Governor of the Tower himself knew! It was a sadness that Richard died from cancer

Peter Dimmock, the television producer (wearing headphones) in the mobile control room, selecting the transmission picture from the preview monitors.

before the era when outstanding commentators were rewarded with a knighthood.

The other television commentators on Coronation day were the late Chester Wilmot, killed in a Comet mid-air explosion, Max Robertson, Michael Henderson and Berkeley Smith. The two latter commentators were also outside broadcasts producers. Following the post-war re-opening of the BBC Television Service we had paid particular attention to developing a team of television outside broadcast commentators, many of whom were also producers. Our mobile equipment was far from reliable in those days and if the commentators were also television producers then at least they understood the technical difficulties. The commentator had to know how to cope with 'talk-back' in his headphones from the producer and not to answer back on the air. Most important of all, however, was the need to cover the unexpected – particularly the loss of a camera at a vital moment. It was difficult to recruit television commentators from radio because they had been taught to keep talking almost non-stop. The television commentator's golden rule was only to speak when they could add to the picture, and 'when in doubt, say nowt'. In fact some of the television commentators nowadays would do well to remember these cardinal rules!

When we combined commentary work with our production duties it was not always because of any talents that we might possess. There was a different incentive. We were categorised as 's.n.f.' which meant 'staff no fee'. This helped the producer with his programme budget; always a meagre one because BBC Radio had the lion's share of the licence revenue.

How did we go about producing a major television outside broadcast? The producer's job is a mixture of art, craft and science in the sense of knowing what the equipment can achieve on the screen. In addition to the all-important skills of the commentator, the producer is completely dependent on the engineering manager and his technicians who, in addition to coping with the mobile outside broadcast control room, cameras, monitor screens, sound lines, hidden microphones and so on, have to set up complicated microwave and cabled vision and sound circuits.

Some people believe that the life of a television outside broadcasts producer simply consists of moving elegantly from one event to another, pointing the cameras and then selecting pictures from any one of the preview monitor screens in front of him in the mobile control room. In a sense this is true, but there is more to it. He must provide a continuous picture for the viewer at home from the best possible vantage point, but at the same time being careful to avoid disorientation by jerking from angle to angle instead of maintaining a smooth continuity of picture.

The actual Coronation service described so vividly in the previous chapter by John Snagge, the radio commentator, presented us with a real challenge. The Engineering Manager, Ben Shaw, and I had an anxious time deciding where the five cameras should be located in the Abbey. Above the West door was an obvious position, as was one high up in the triforium together with side view cameras. The real problem was how to position a camera to cover the service from the centre of the organ loft above the choir screen. The difficulty was that the whole area was occupied by the massive orchestra under the direction of Dr William McKie. He was most co-operative and allowed us to place a camera in front of the orchestra, hidden in the balustrade.

The next problem was how to operate it without distracting either the musicians or those participating in the service. The Ministry of Works came to our rescue. We cut a hole in the floor and immediately assigned our smallest cameraman, 'Bud' Flanagan, to the important task of operating it. This camera was in fact absolutely vital to our coverage of the ceremony itself and provided some of the most stunning and memorable pictures of the Coronation service which had never, of course, been covered on live television. There was one further problem with this camera. Because of its proximity to the service 'Bud' Flanagan could not use his customary talk-back microphone to answer any of my production questions from the control room. Countless peers and peeresses seated in the transepts were no doubt astonished to see a diminutive figure in white tie and tails in front of the orchestra constantly either touching his nose or tweaking his ear. This meant either 'yes' or 'no'! I could see him from one of the other cameras mounted high in the triforium.

The production was rather like televising a play. The Earl Marshal, the Duke of Norfolk, had kindly allowed me to watch all the individual segment rehearsals in the Abbey. He would not, however, allow the television cameras to be on. As a result, John Vernon, my Assistant Producer, Gwen Foyle, our indefatigable and priceless Production Assistant, and I had to prepare a very detailed shooting script with provision for any unexpected camera failures. In fact, on the day none occurred and I still believe that there was a divine intervention to make sure that all went well.

One aspect of the service had troubled me during the early music rehearsals and I learned later that John Snagge – who was giving the BBC radio commentary in the Abbey – shared my concern. It was proposed that a rather ordinary sounding piece of music written by the Master of The Queen's Music should be played as The Queen and Prince Philip processed down the aisle towards the West door after the service. From a theatrical production point of view, this was a crucial moment of the broadcast. The Queen had been crowned, and to capture what I thought would be an outstanding head-on picture of Her Majesty, we had concealed one of our cameras above the door. It did, however, need a really patriotic and emotional piece of music to make the major impact on the screen that we wanted to achieve. I mentioned this to the Earl Marshal and Dr William McKie who asked what I would suggest. I replied, 'How about "Land of Hope and Glory"?' Apparently John Snagge had made the same suggestion and so we had our way. At that particular moment in the broadcast there wasn't a dry eye in the control room or in front of any television set throughout the land, as the music swelled to a crescendo with The Queen looking ravishingly beautiful in a spectactular close-up as she approached the West door. Thank goodness the Earl Marshal had shared our sense of 'theatre'.

There was another moment during the service which was both emotionally exciting and could also be said to have provided a sense of theatre. This was when Prince Charles, then four and a half years old, was brought to the Abbey just in time to witness the moment that Her Majesty was crowned. The Earl Marshal had arranged for me to be tipped off in advance about this secret plan so as to enable a television close-up to be transmitted of our future King peeping over the front of a box from which he had a perfect view of this historic moment.

I also had with me in the control room adjoining the Abbey, the Reverend Francis House, Head of BBC Religious Broadcasting. He was able to give us invaluable advice on the special religious significance of the Coronation service and also helped no end in establishing a very cordial and rewarding relationship with both the Dean and the Archbishop.

The Queen as seen by a BBC *camera.* It was the first time television cameras had been allowed inside the Abbey for a Coronation.

There was, of course, a full rehearsal in the Abbey. We covered this and telerecorded it. As we had not had permission to use our cameras in the Abbey before this, we took the opportunity to experiment and see whether the script and camera angles that we had prepared in advance would work in practice. We were taking a great deal of our sound coverage from radio, and they were experimenting too with various microphone locations. The overall result on the screen, which we telerecorded, was pretty chaotic. So much so, in fact, that George Barnes, the Director of Television – a very charming academic and radio man, who did not really understand, or much care about, television – was so disturbed by what he had seen on his office screen during the rehearsal that he telephoned Cecil McGivern, the Controller of BBC Television Programmes, for his opinion. McGivern apparently was also rather concerned but hoped that a seemingly disjointed rehearsal would prove the old adage that 'it would be all right on the night' to be true!

In fact the whole day's television coverage went without any serious hitch. George Barnes was given a knighthood by The Queen in his office at the Lime Grove studios where Her Majesty went some time later to see the television recording. The Queen asked for me to be awarded the Coronation Medal as a tribute to everyone in Television Outside Broadcasts who had worked so hard to ensure the success of the television coverage.

Finally, I must mention the vital role of the Post Office. Their Engineering Division, combined with that of the BBC, provided some 1300 additional sound circuits as well as over 100 extra vision circuits, to ensure that sound and vision were well received in the British Isles and also beamed successfully across the Channel via live television links to the continental television organisations, including Berlin which at that time was 100 miles east of the Iron Curtain. Telerecordings (there was no videotape in those days) were flown to Canada and the United States.

A central television control room and vision switching centre was established in Broadcasting House to co-ordinate the television pictures from the various locations en route to the transmitters, and

BBC *Television stayed on air to cover the fireworks display on the River Thames which took place later that evening.*

to ensure smooth hand-overs from one mobile unit to another as the day progressed.

It was an unforgettable experience for all of us fortunate enough to be part of such a major event, and in recalling some of it I may have wandered from the Editor's brief. Nevertheless I hope that it may have given a small insight into the work of a television outside broadcast producer at a major live event in those early post-war years. We were very much 'Jack of all trades' but not, we hope, 'Master of none'.

THE ANNUAL CALENDAR OF ROYAL EVENTS

TOM FLEMING, OBE

Tom Fleming gave his first commentary for radio on a royal event in 1950. He has commentated regularly since then at most of the annual events which include Trooping the Colour, the Royal Maundy service, the Remembrance Day service at the Cenotaph in Whitehall, and the Christmas Day service at Windsor Castle. He has worked for both BBC Television and BBC Radio and has acquired a detailed knowledge of the meaning and significance of the annual royal events that are broadcast.

EACH YEAR, BBC TELEVISION AND RADIO cover a number of royal events that are written into the traditional pattern of our national life. These occasions are now shared by millions of viewers and listeners throughout the British Isles, where in previous generations they could be witnessed only by those who were present by invitation or choice, and those who were prepared to make what, in many cases, would be a long and possibly 'once in a lifetime' journey to London. For it is in the southern capital that most of these events take place.

The exception is the Royal Maundy service which takes place annually in the early spring, on the Thursday of Holy Week – known as Maundy Thursday. For over sixty years from 1890, it was the custom to hold this act of divine worship, which incorporates the ancient custom of distributing gifts from the Sovereign, in Westminster Abbey. In the three Coronation years (1911, 1937 and 1953), St Paul's was used. During the reign of our present Queen the distribution has more often taken place in a cathedral or church somewhere outside London. This 'new' tradition began in 1957, when the service was held in St Albans. The ceremony had not taken place out of the capital for two centuries. Since then Her Majesty has travelled from Carlisle to Salisbury, and from Durham to Winchester, a cathedral which dates from 1079, only some hundred years before the Royal Maundy distribution was instituted.

The service has been in the calendar since the reign of King Edward I. The ceremony became an occasion for the public display of royal charity and humility. At the Last Supper, on the eve of the crucifixion, Jesus washed the feet of his disciples and said to them, 'I give you a new commandment; Love one another; as I have loved you.' (The Latin word for a commandment is 'mandatum', from which the expression 'Maundy' is derived.) That sentence from St John's Gospel is read each year at the beginning of the 'Office for the Royal Maundy', as the service is formally known.

The Sovereign, in earlier times, gave alms and gifts of food, drink and clothing to the poor, as well as washing and kissing their feet. From the beginning of the fifteenth century, the number of those receiving gifts and money has been related to the years of the Sovereign's life, and whereas once a king gave only to poor men, and a queen to poor women, since the eighteenth century an equal number of men and women have been chosen each year as the recipients. In the sixteenth century, Queen Mary gave away her gown to the neediest and oldest of the poor women present. In the same century, Queen Elizabeth I decided not to follow suit, but in lieu gave a sum of money (twenty shillings) to each of the assembled poor. She also agreed to wash their feet only after they had been given a preliminary rinse in

*The Queen Mother walks in the gardens of her childhood
home at St Paul's Walden Bury, Hertfordshire with Tom Fleming
during the filming of* In This Your Honour.
*Tom Fleming wrote, narrated and was the executive producer
of this eightieth-birthday portrait.*

sweet-scented water by the Lord High Almoner and the Sub-Almoner! The washing of the feet was abandoned around 1730. However, the Lord High Almoner and his assistants still have linen towels worn over the right shoulder and tied round the waist as a remembrance of that ancient custom, and nosegays of sweet-smelling herbs and spring flowers are still carried by the main participants, including The Queen.

It was also around 1730 that the Sovereign ceased to attend the Office of the Royal Maundy in person. The Queen's grandfather, King George V, revived the tradition in 1932, after a break of two centuries, and in 1935, The Queen (as Princess Elizabeth) attended the service when she was only nine, with her mother, the Duchess of York (now Queen Elizabeth The Queen Mother). The Queen's father, King George VI, attended the ceremony seven times during his reign, but since her accession Queen Elizabeth II has missed very few Royal Maundy distributions. Recipients are now chosen because of some Christian service they have given (often unobtrusively and quietly) to either the Church or the community where they live. They are all over sixty-five, and some have been sixty-five for twenty years and more! The gifts they receive are symbols only, and certainly not charity, but they are always highly prized.

The Queen is attended by her Bodyguard of The Yeomen of the Guard, in their scarlet Tudor tunics and 'low-crowned' velvet hats. Three Yeomen carry on these flat-topped hats the Maundy dish and the two 'fish' dishes (huge silver-gilt plates brought for the occasion from the Tower of London) containing the leather purses which hold the Royal Maundy gifts. They place them on the nave altar. After the reading of the first lesson (usually by His Royal Highness The Duke of Edinburgh when he is present) the first distribution of 'alms' is made. The Queen walks the length of the nave accompanied by the officials of the Royal Almonry, the Secretary, the Sub-Almoner and the Lord High Almoner, (when I last described the scene he was six feet six inches 'high' – the Right Reverend Richard Say, Bishop of Rochester!) She gives the first purses of Tudor green, with short white leather strings, to the women recipients. Each purse contains a gift of three pounds (in new pound coins) in lieu of items of clothing given

The Queen distributes the Royal Maundy in Westminster Abbey. Recipients are now chosen because of some Christian service they have given to the Church or community where they live.

in earlier years. In the second distribution, which follows the second lesson, each recipient receives two further purses. One is red with long white strings and contains one pound (to honour Queen Elizabeth I's pledge to redeem her gown for twenty shillings) and an additional one pound fifty pence, also in normal currency, in lieu of the provisions once given (a gallon of beer, a quart of wine, six penny rolls and a quantity of fish which included red herrings!) The other is a white purse with long red strings and it is this which contains the much cherished, specially minted Maundy coins. In one, two, three and four pence denominations (and the equivalent number of pennies to the years of The Queen's age in that year), they are made of 92.5 per cent pure silver – à link to the silver penny, which dates back to AD 760 and was called the 'sterling', so giving our currency its name.

It is a simple and moving annual event in which the practice of humility is at the heart of a tradition which takes us, in time, almost half-way back to the origins of our Christian faith and links us – through the lives of ordinary men and women, rewarded in token at the hand of their Sovereign – to all the quiet goodness that goes on in our world, unnoticed and seeking no reward.

The years of The Queen's life are marked on two other occasions in the year – her birthdays. She has two! Her Majesty was born on 21 April 1926. On the anniversary of that day, flags are flown on public buildings and a royal salute of sixty-two guns is fired at the Tower of London. Otherwise, the event is one for private celebration.

On a Saturday in June (usually the second), the Official Birthday of the Sovereign is celebrated by perhaps the most spectacular ceremonial in the world – the Queen's Birthday Parade, or Trooping the Colour, on Horse Guards Parade in London. This open space between Whitehall and St James's Park was once the site of the Tilt Yard of Henry VIII's Whitehall Palace, where tourneys were held and knights in armour jousted. In the Birthday Parade, the seven regiments of the Household Division, all of which have close links with the Crown, salute their royal Colonel-in-Chief. But it is the five regiments of Footguards (Grenadier, Coldstream, Scots, Irish and Welsh) that perform the central ceremonial.

One of the eight serving battalions of these five regiments takes it in turn, annually, to honour the Queen's Colour, which it has been given by Her Majesty, by trooping it through the ranks in the presence of The Queen. The two regiments of Household Cavalry, the Life Guards and the Blues and Royals, provide the Sovereign's Escort. They carry a Sovereign's Standard (the only standard, guidon or colour in the British Army to bear the royal coat of arms) and are accompanied by their two Mounted Guards. There are over 200 horses on parade; 179 of them come from the Household Cavalry Barracks in Hyde Park. The others are ridden by the four royal colonels: the Duke of Edinburgh (Grenadier Guards), the Prince of Wales (Welsh Guards), the Duke of Kent (Scots Guards) and the Grand-Duke of Luxembourg (Irish Guards); by the Colonels of the other three Household Division Regiments, the attendant officers of The Queen's procession, and the four Footguards officers of the Parade: the Field Officer-in-Brigade-Waiting (who commands the Parade), the Brigade Major (a lieutenant-colonel who during his three year appointment is the 'executive producer' of the Parade), the Major of the Parade, and the Adjutant.

For the Guardsmen, there are ten weeks of intense preparation on the square at Chelsea Barracks, under the eagle eyes of drill sergeants and to the husky roar of sergeant-majors. On the day itself, reveille is at 6.30 a.m. There is an obligatory session of physical training, a good breakfast, a final inspection, and a three-mile march to the famous parade ground. When all the eight Guards, each of three officers and seventy non-commissioned officers and guardsmen, are formed up (Nos 1 to 5 face the Horseguards Archway, Nos 6 to 8 front the Old Admiralty building), and the 360 musicians in the Massed Bands of all five Guards regiments are in position with the back gardens of Downing Street behind them, there are already nearly 1000 on parade. No. 3 Guard opens to allow The Queen Mother's carriage (a barouche from the Royal Mews) to pass through. Often she has one or two of her great-grandchildren with her, to the delight of the 7000 spectators in the stands. She is greeted with a Royal Salute as her small procession, led by two royal grooms, crosses the parade ground and disappears under the Archway. A few minutes later she will re-appear at the central window. The small room from which she will watch the proceedings was once the Duke of Wellington's office, and his desk is still there.

Ten minutes later, at precisely eleven o'clock, Her Majesty The Queen arrives, accompanied by a Sovereign's Escort of Household

Cavalry and preceded by the Massed Mounted Bands. The hour rings out from the central clock tower on Horse Guards. Before the day of Big Ben, this was the most accurate clock in London, and there is no truth in the rumour that a duty Guardsman holds back the striker until the moment of the royal arrival! When The Queen rode side-saddle to her Birthday Parade each year, in the scarlet tunic of the appropriate regiment, she always saluted first the Colour to be trooped, posted with sentries in front and to the left of No. 6 Guard and then, as she approached the Horse Guards Archway, saluted her mother, Queen Elizabeth, watching from the window above. It was in 1986 – the year of her sixtieth birthday – that The Queen rode on the black mare Burmese for the last time. In 1987 as she drove from the Palace in a light carriage called 'the ivory-mounted phaeton' which had been built for Queen Victoria in 1842, she glanced thoughtfully at Burmese on police duty just outside the Palace railings. She had been a gift from the Royal Canadian Mounted Police in 1969, and had carried The Queen safely and surely that very year and for seventeen subsequent Birthday Parades.

There are five main parts to this Parade: the Inspection; the Troop (a musical marching display by the Massed Bands); the solemn collection of the Colour by the 'Escort' (as the No. 1 Guard to the right of the line is called) and the Trooping of the Colour through the ranks of the other seven Guards; the March Past of the Footguards in slow and quick time; lastly, the Walk and Trot Past of the Household Cavalry (included within the Parade since the first year of The Queen's reign). Each, in its own way, is memorable.

When The Queen inspects the eight Guards and the Sovereign's Escort, I find myself realising that she first rode on the Birthday Parade, by her father's side, in June 1947. She was appointed Colonel of the Grenadier Guards in 1942, at the age of sixteen. No detail of

LEFT: *Burmese was a present from the Royal Canadian Mounted Police in 1969 and carried The Queen at every Trooping the Colour ceremony for eighteen years.*

uniform or dressing escapes her knowledgeable eye. The music of the Massed Bands, and the unique spin-wheel marching formation which they perform as they continue to play and in which they change direction completely by pivoting on the centre, are highlights for me.

Then one never fails to be moved as the Colour is trooped in slow time through the ranks. This rite has been observed for 300 years. It originated so that soldiers might become familiar with their own Colour, and recognise it as a rallying point in the smoke and dust of battle. At night the Colour was lodged in a safe billet, and in the morning paraded with honour to its place among the assembled troops. In time the Colour came to represent the ongoing life of the regiment itself, to be defended, treasured and respected at all times.

The March Past of the Guards is always an unforgettable sight: the long lines of black bearskins and scarlet tunics, the shiny boots rising and falling in unison, as each Guard marks time on the corners, and regimental march gives way to regimental march as the saluting base is approached.

Lastly, those magnificent skewbald and piebald drum horses with their priceless silver kettle drums (each weighs nearly a hundredweight) move to the centre of the arena. The drum horses and the Mounted Bands of both Household Cavalry regiments have paraded together only since 1971. Is there a more splendid sight anywhere than the Troopers of the Household Cavalry in their gleaming cuirasses and glistening helmets, their white and red whalebone plumes bobbing up and down, their sword blades flashing in the sun, as their handsomely groomed black horses (already on duty by this time for two and a half hours) raise the dust and joyously and spontaneously break into the trot as they hear the trumpeter (on his grey horse) sound the call? It is when the cavalry have departed that the crowds who have stood under the trees of St James's Park and The Mall since early morning see the once-a-year sight of The Queen driving home at the head of her Guards. In 1988, all the regiments of Footguards were on parade. This is unlikely to happen again in this century.

A man paid seven hundred pounds some years ago to fly from Australia, see the Birthday Parade, and fly home next day. 'It was

The Royal Family on the balcony of Buckingham Palace watching the RAF *fly-past after Trooping the Colour.*

worth every penny!' he is reported as saying. Well, I've seen the Parade fifty-four times (counting rehearsals) and I agree.

There have, of course, been some heart-stopping moments in two decades of watching. In 1972, the Birthday Parade took place a few days after the death of the Duke of Windsor. The Queen and all the officers on parade wore black mourning bands. At the beginning of the Parade there was a roll of drums, a silence, another roll of drums, then a lament played on the pipes for the king whose birthday was celebrated only once on Horse Guards, on 23 June 1936. That was, in fact, his *real* birthday; Edward VIII was forty-two on that very day. By his forty-third birthday, he had abdicated, and his brother had been crowned King at Westminster Abbey.

On 16 June 1979, Earl Mountbatten of Burma rode as Colonel of the Life Guards, as usual. He had received that appointment fourteen years previously and, excellent horseman that he was, he had become a familiar figure on the Birthday Parade, riding low in the saddle, his breastplate scarcely visible under campaign medals. A few short weeks after that Parade, he was killed by a terrorist bomb in Ireland. In his funeral procession, 'Dolly', the horse he had ridden on the Birthday Parade, was led, riderless, across Horse Guards and through the Archway. 'Colonel Dicky's' boots, reversed, were in the stirrups.

Only two years after that tragic happening, as The Queen turned from The Mall into Horse Guards approach road, at a few minutes to eleven and just before the Birthday Parade on Saturday 13 June 1981, a young man in the crowd fired 'blanks' from a starting pistol. He was grabbed by a Lance Corporal in the Scots Guards, who was a 'street-liner', hauled over the barrier and handed over to the police. The Queen scarcely lost her composure for a second, calmed old Burmese with a pat on the neck, and rode on as though nothing had happened. The other horses seemed more upset by police officers rushing across the approach road in front of them, than by the incident itself. The Parade carried on without any interruption, and an hour and a few minutes later, The Queen rode back round the same corner, and home along The Mall, leading her Guards to Buckingham Palace through cheering crowds who were quite unaware that anything untoward had happened.

On Saturday 12 June 1982, there was again a one-minute silence after the first royal salute of the Parade and when the Guards had ordered arms. This was to remember members of the Armed Forces and the Merchant Navy who were on active service in the South Atlantic. The First Battalion, Welsh Guards, who had trooped their Colour the previous year and should have been on parade that morning, were serving with the Falklands Task Force. So were two troops of the Blues and Royals, and the Second Battalion, Scots Guards. We had heard a rumour in the commentary box that something pretty awful had happened, but, of course, nothing could be said at that stage. Within forty-eight hours, news of the *Sir Galahad* attack four days previously was being released, and later that year I attended a memorial service in Llandaff Cathedral for thirty-nine men of the Welsh Guards who had been killed. Their Colonel, the Prince of Wales, was present. Some of the widows looked so young, scarcely out of school. They had brought their babies and small toddlers with them. It was heart-breaking.

During the summer there are other annual events in London regularly attended by members of the Royal Family. In May, the Chelsea Flower Show is held in the grounds of the Royal Hospital, and in July, the Royal Tournament at Earls Court raises money for Service charities, and both these occasions receive considerable coverage on radio and television. However, three events of national significance occur later in the year, and all in the month of November.

The State Opening of Parliament can happen at other times of the year, or even more than once in the same year if there has been a change of Government, but usually it simply marks the opening of the new parliamentary session in November. It is a day of high symbolism and pageantry which encapsulates most of the ground rules for our particular kind of parliamentary democracy under the Crown. When The Queen drives in state from Buckingham Palace to Westminster in the Irish State Coach with a Sovereign's Escort of Household Cavalry, she has been preceded by the regalia which have previously been collected from the Tower of London, and travel in a carriage (usually Queen Alexandra's State Coach) with an Escort of a Corporal-of-Horse and six troopers from the Household Cavalry. The Imperial State Crown is carried by the Comptroller of the Lord Chamberlain's Office, the Cap of Maintenance (an emblem of royal dignity made of crimson velvet trimmed with ermine) is carried by the Assistant Comptroller, and the Sword of State by a Gentleman Usher. Two Sergeants at Arms, with their maces, accompany them. The troops lining the streets pay compliments to the small regalia procession as well as to the State Procession of the Sovereign. On her arrival at the Palace of Westminster, The Queen is welcomed by a Royal Salute from the Guard of Honour, the Royal Standard is raised on the Victoria Tower, and gun salutes thunder across London. The Earl

ABOVE: *Televising the State Opening of Parliament. Black Rod moves towards the door of the House of Commons which is slammed in his face. He knocks three times and is admitted.*

LEFT: *The Queen, in the House of Lords, reaches into her handbag for her glasses to read 'The most gracious speech from the Throne' during the State Opening of Parliament.*

Marshal of England and the Lord Great Chamberlain, who is Keeper of the Royal Palace of Westminster, receive Her Majesty at the Sovereign's Entrance and she is escorted up the Royal Staircase to the Robing Chamber through a Guard of Honour of dismounted troopers of the Household Cavalry, in full dress, with drawn swords. A detachment of ten Yeomen of the Guard, with lanterns, has already searched the cellars, having caught Guido Fawkes there up to no good in 1605, on the fifth of another November!

The Queen, robed and wearing the Imperial State Crown, then moves slowly in procession through the Royal Gallery to the House of Lords, preceded by the heralds and pursuivants in their rich tabards, members of her Household, the Kings of Arms, the Lord Privy Seal, the Lord High Chancellor (Keeper of the Great Seal), the Lord President of the Council, the Earl Marshal and the Lord Great Chamberlain (walking backwards) and the Sword of State and the Cap of Maintenance carried by peers. In Their Lordships' House, the peers and peeresses are in parliamentary robes, the Lords Spiritual in ecclesiastical robes, the Judges of the High Court of Justice in judicial robes and full-bottomed wigs. When The Queen is seated on the throne, the Duke of Edinburgh sits on her left, and the Prince of Wales on her right. It is at this point that the Commons are summoned by the Sovereign's Messenger, the Gentleman Usher of the Black Rod. The door of the Commons is slammed in his face. He knocks three times and is admitted. The Commons are exercising their right to exclude anyone from their Chamber except the Sovereign's Messenger. Charles I, three and a half centuries ago, tried to arrest five Members of Parliament. No sovereign now enters the House of Commons. An exception was The Queen's father, King George VI, who inspected the Chamber after its restoration from bomb damage suffered in the Second World War. The members of the House of Commons comply with the Sovereign's command (without haste) and, led by the Speaker and the Sergeant at Arms carrying his mace, they walk to 'the other place', chatting amongst themselves to show that they are not over-awed by coming to the House of Peers. They stand at the far end of the Chamber from the throne (where there is room for only a third of the 650 Members of Parliament) to hear the Sovereign read 'The Most Gracious Speech from the Throne' (a summary of the Government of the day's intentions for the coming session, compiled by the Cabinet). At the end of this speech The Queen says, 'I pray that the blessing of Almighty God may rest upon your counsels', and Parliament (from 'parlement' meaning speaking or discussion) is formally open.

The Sunday nearest to 11 November is designated Remembrance Sunday. On that morning representatives of the three Services, of the Commonwealth nations, of both Houses of Parliament and of the main religious denominations in Britain are joined around the Cenotaph in Whitehall by thousands of ex-Service men and women, and by countless ordinary citizens for a service of remembrance. At one minute to eleven, Her Majesty The Queen, usually accompanied by at least four royal princes, walks to the centre of the roadway to lead the nation's homage to the dead of the two World Wars, and those killed on active service since. As eleven o'clock strikes from Big Ben at Westminster, a gun fires on Horse Guards Parade and two minutes of silence and stillness descend on Whitehall. It is an unforgettable moment in what for me has become perhaps the most meaningful of all the annual events.

Like most that is best in British traditions, what happens on that Sunday in November at Whitehall came about almost by chance. The First World War ended at the eleventh hour of the eleventh day of the eleventh month. It was an Australian journalist living in Britain who first had the idea of re-creating each year the silence that fell along the Western Front as the guns ceased firing, and of setting two minutes apart from the hurly-burly of life to remember the awful cost in human lives of war. The suggestion was put to King George V who gave the proposal his approval. The Cenotaph (or 'empty tomb'), designed by Sir Edwin Lutyens, was a temporary structure built for the Peace Parade of 1919 as a focus for the nation's pride and remembrance. It was heaped with banks of fresh flowers (the Flanders poppies were to come in later years) in tribute to the 1 114 814 men of the British Empire killed in the Great War. It caught the imagination of the British people and, by public demand, it was rebuilt using Portland

Stone on the same spot in the street of government as a constant reminder of what war means in human terms. There are no names upon the Cenotaph and no religious symbols. Only three words were chiselled from the stone: THE GLORIOUS DEAD; and in Roman numerals two dates: 1914 and 1919. It was unveiled on 11 November 1920 by The Queen's grandfather, as the body of the Unknown Warrior lay on a gun-carriage beside it, awaiting burial that same morning in Westminster Abbey. Only twenty-five years later, the dates of another war were inscribed on the Cenotaph: 1939 and 1945. Another 580 000 British and Commonwealth men and women had been killed in the world-wide conflict which we call the Second World War.

Remembrance Sunday is more of a 'people' day than a 'Royal' day. The Queen lays her wreath on behalf of all of us. But the Royal Family is not immune from bereavement and human loss. Prince Andrew for some years now has laid a wreath in the distinctive colours of the South Atlantic for those who died in the Falklands campaign, in which he served. The Duke of Kent and his brother also lay wreaths. Their father, The Queen's uncle, was killed in an aircrash on active service with the Royal Air Force in 1942. The present Duke was six, and Prince Michael a few weeks old. The Queen Mother was fourteen on the very day the Great War began. She lost a brother, another was wounded, and a third taken prisoner. In the Second World War she lost a nephew.

As a broadcaster, Remembrance Sunday has been part of my life for nearly thirty years. The veterans of the Second World War are now older than the veterans of the Great War were when first I described the scene. But the paradox is that where ten years ago 3500 ex-Servicemen marched past the Cenopath, today upwards of 9000 turn their eyes to the simple white stone memorial. They include always the war-blinded from St Dunstan's, their arms linked together,

RIGHT: *The Queen lays a wreath at the Cenotaph in Whitehall. The Sunday nearest to 11 November is designated Remembrance Sunday.*

and the disabled ex-Servicemen in their flotilla of wheelchairs. And now there are almost as many women as men, and at last the war widows take their rightful place.

The evening before, in the Albert Hall, the Royal British Legion holds its Festival of Remembrance. Most of the Royal Family are present. It is a nostalgic occasion. The old war-time songs are sung with gusto. But there is also an intensely moving climax to the evening when the words of Binyon's 'For the Fallen' are spoken: 'They shall not grow old as we that are left grow old ...' and in silence tens of thousands of red poppy petals flutter down from the darkness above. 'For every petal, a life laid down.'

For those too young to have been alive when the things we remember each November happened, it is still a worthwhile time to pause, to reflect on what has been, and to dedicate their lives anew to creating the better, happier world for which we all long, and for which so many young men and women fought and died in the first half of the twentieth century. Sometimes that world seems almost within grasp. But twelve months later you can be forgiven for wondering if the human race will ever learn the lessons of history.

There is one more royal 'happening', at the very end of the year, which the BBC is allowed to broadcast only every sixth year. On the morning of Christmas Day the entire Royal Family attends Matins in St George's Chapel within Windsor Castle. It is always a happy and informal occasion. All the BBC riggers, electricians, engineers, cameramen and production team have given up part of their Christmas to be there and make the broadcast happen. There are carols, there is holly from Home Park, and sometimes even snow. (And there is no public transport for two days!) John Gilpin, one of our senior stage managers, who is often with me in the commentary box on these occasions, has a most thoughtful wife who never forgets a flask of coffee (for two) and has even been known to provide a mince pie for an exiled Scottish commentator. But we don't 'hang around' more than necessary. For broadcasters, as for 'the Royals', Christmas is essentially a family day.

THE INVESTITURE OF HIS ROYAL HIGHNESS THE PRINCE OF WALES

ALUN WILLIAMS, OBE

On 1 July 1969 in Caernarfon Castle, Prince Charles was invested as His Royal Highness The Prince of Wales. Thousands of people flocked to the Castle to see the ceremony, and millions more heard it on radio and watched it on television. Alun Williams had been working for the BBC for over twenty years and most of his work had been with the Outside Broadcasts Department either commentating at sporting events or royal occasions. The Investiture of the Prince of Wales was to be one of the greatest royal events that had occurred in Wales in the twentieth century and Alun Williams recalls the moment Her Majesty The Queen announced the date to the world.

THE EMPIRE GAMES WERE HELD in Cardiff in 1958 and The Queen was to be at the closing ceremony. A warm Welsh welcome awaited her and there was naturally great disappointment in the Principality when it was announced that she was not well and would be unable to attend.

Then we heard that, although she could not be there in person, her speech declaring the closure of the great international event would be recorded in advance and played to the great crowds at Cardiff Arms Park and, of course, the listeners and viewers all over the world; but few people knew how she would end that speech, for the announcement made by Her Majesty was one of the best kept secrets in broadcasting history. The tape recording was made in Windsor Castle and normal procedure would then be to play it 'down the line' from Broadcasting House in London to BBC headquarters in Cardiff, but this would have revealed the contents to a great number of engineers, technicians and others.

So, under an impenetrable cloak of secrecy (and in order, perhaps, to make it a truly international 'transfer'!) a BBC driver brought the tape to a pre-arranged rendezvous near Gloucester and was met there by a Welsh driver who brought the precious parcel to Cardiff.

I was the commentator for the BBC Radio coverage of the closing ceremony, but knew nothing apart from what I was told by Charles Max-Muller, the Head of Outside Broadcasts, about five minutes before we went on the air: 'There'll be an unexpected announcement by Her Majesty towards the end of the speech and I think your reaction will make better listening material if it's completely spontaneous.'

So commentators and crowds alike were completely unaware of what was to follow until we heard The Queen's voice:

'I want to take this opportunity of speaking to all Welsh people, not only in this arena, but wherever they may be. The British Empire and Commonwealth Games in the capital, together with all the activities of the Festival of Wales, have made this a memorable year for the Principality. I have therefore decided to mark it further by an act which will, I hope, give as much pleasure to all Welshmen as it does to me. I intend to create my son Charles, Prince of Wales today. When he is grown up I will present him to you at Caernarfon.'

The tape operator had been well briefed, stopped the machine after the word 'today', and waited until the great roar of the crowd had died down before restarting the tape for the next sentence.

Eleven years later the Prince, in a BBC interview, revealed that he had heard the announcement as a nine-year-old schoolboy in the Headmaster's study at his school in Cheam along with some of his school friends, and that he was 'acutely embarrassed' when he heard the great cheer from the Cardiff crowd, and 'rather bewildered' when all the others turned and looked at him in amazement!

In May and June of 1969 I was visiting New Zealand and Australia covering the tour by the Welsh rugby team, and before the second international match in Auckland was invited to the television studios to comment not on rugby, but on a film of Prince Charles addressing his audience at the Welsh Youth League (Urdd Gobaith Cymru) Eisteddfod in fluent Welsh. It was obvious that his term as a student at Aberystwyth University had paid handsome dividends.

A week later in Sydney, Australia on 19 June I was preparing for the test match there and looking forward with pleasure to a few days in Fiji before returning to Wales for the Investiture, when a cable arrived from London informing me that I would have to forego the match in Suva and return to London immediately after the Sydney game. This was so that I might have enough time to prepare for my commentary on the Investiture at Caernarfon Castle on 1 July. I had my leg pulled by the Welsh full-back J. P. R. Williams over this, for he was taking part in the ceremony in a procession representing the youth of Wales but he was going to Fiji as well!

The Welsh speaking members of the team were unanimous in their praise of the Prince's speech at the Eisteddfod, but when we returned home we soon found that there were some who were not happy about the ceremony. Decorations were torn down, English signs painted out, and hundreds gathered at Cilmeri to register their protest. They met at the granite memorial to Llewellyn, the last native Prince of Wales, who was killed there in 1282, and Dafydd Iwan, Chairman of the Welsh Language Society said, 'We are paying tribute to the last real Prince of Wales and expressing our opposition to the Investiture. We regard it as an insult to have an English Prince thrust on us. Charles has no moral right to the title.'

We wondered how His Royal Highness felt about the opposition to the ceremony, and an interview broadcast at the time, in which he answered questions put to him by Cliff Michelmore and Brian Connell, revealed his feelings, and a character far removed from the 'acutely embarrassed' schoolboy in Cheam eleven years previously.

Q: 'Were you lonely at Aberystwyth?'

A: 'One has to remember that I am in a slightly different position from several other people. Out of a certain necessity I've been more lonely – I haven't made a lot of friends – I haven't been to a lot of parties and I've had a lot of other things to do. I've been around Wales a lot, and essentially it is, compared with other people's lives, more lonely.'

Q: 'You've also learned the Welsh language. Did you find that difficult, because most English tongues find that difficult to get round?'

A: 'All languages are difficult, but there are certain things, like the double 'l's which are fairly difficult, except that I went to Llanelli not long ago and the Mayor said, "Can you say 'Llanelli'?" and I said "Llanelli" and he wiped the saliva out of his eye and said, "Well done!" There is a way of doing it, you put your tongue in a certain place and blow. I haven't found it too bad because I can imitate accents reasonably well and it's helped to speak Welsh.'

Q: 'When you came to Wales there was quite a lot of strong anti-English nationalist feeling. Were you at all apprehensive?'

A: 'Yes I was. I think this is due very much to the Press ... naturally misgivings built up and one had an exaggerated picture of the whole situation.

'I want to meet the student nationalists. They did offer to

meet me in the local milk bar, but I thought I'd choose my own particular site for that, but at the moment they're involved with exams and they haven't demonstrated too much. I've had some very interesting talks with Mr Millward my Welsh tutor, and he has enlightened me a great deal about nationalist aims, ideas and policies.'

Q: 'What interpretation do you put on your motto "Ich dien" – "I serve"?'
A: 'Exactly that. It's a marvellous motto to have and that is the basis of one's job: to serve other people. If you have a sense of duty, and I like to think I have, then you can be of service.'

Q: 'Do you believe yourself to be exploited by politicians with the Investiture?'
A: 'No. I love the cry that I'm a political tool. I know I'm not exploited by politicians. Perhaps the Investiture was encouraged and pushed by certain politicians, but not blatantly – it's a very convenient cry for those who are anti-Investiture.'

Q: 'What will the Investiture mean to you?'
A: 'Quite a lot. On the whole I will be glad when it's over, but that doesn't mean that I shan't get any meaning out of it . . . . I like to think that it symbolises "Ich dien" . . . . It will be an exhausting but enjoyable day. I do enjoy ceremonies and I think the British do them so very well, particularly with the Duke of Norfolk.'

Apart from the Duke, Lord Snowdon played an essential part in the staging of the ceremony and the design involved. He decided that the simplicity of Caernarfon Castle should speak for itself, and that he would avoid introducing any elements which would appeal only to the audience there present, and would be guided by consideration for the millions of viewers all over the world.

There were, inevitably, differences of opinion in the planning stages. Lord Snowdon, the Constable of the Castle, was respectfully informed by the officer commanding the Household Cavalry that two banners which he had hung opposite the Water Gate would, in a breeze, startle his mounts just as The Queen was descending from her carriage. The Constable agreed and they were removed. The Welsh conductors of the singing asked for elaborate podia, but as these would have prevented a full view of the distinguished members of the chorus and orchestra, they were asked to do without them: they agreed. The Duke of Norfolk wanted a striped awning along the entire length of the royal walk to keep The Queen dry, but here again the audience would have been deprived of a satisfactory view of the procession so the project was dropped.

We were allowed to visit the Castle on the Sunday and saw that, indeed, the designers of the background for the pageant had avoided any over-elaboration and had allowed this great grey fortress to speak for itself.

The most eye-catching addition to the normal scene was a flat circle of slate, quarried in Dinorwic at the foot of the Llanberis Pass in Snowdonia. On this dais stood three slate thrones designed so simply that they would not have looked out of place in Stonehenge. On each throne was a scarlet cushion, so that against the green of the grass we saw the contrasting scarlet of the cushions and the dark blue of the slate. Above this centrepiece, instead of the traditional striped awning, which would have dimmed the light on the central characters of the drama, a large canopy was made of perspex acrylic on a steel frame, so that a medieval look was achieved with modern materials; nor were any traditional red carpets allowed.

On the Sunday night I asked three of my London colleagues, Robert Hudson, Raymond Baxter and Arthur Phillips, to join me in Siloh Chapel for the evening service. They readily agreed and although the entire proceedings were conducted in Welsh, they felt that the visit had added considerably to the atmosphere which we were all 'soaking up' in preparation for the big day. As is customary in Welsh non-conformist services they were all greeted by name by the chief deacon from the 'set fawr', the 'big seat' below the pulpit, (I had quietly briefed him before the service), and they joined in the singing of the Welsh hymns with gusto.

Thousands of guests were expected at the ceremony and hotel accommodation was fully booked for miles around. In its wisdom, the BBC had taken over one of the university hostels at nearby Bangor and our stay there provided a very happy reunion for the outside broadcasters and commentators. Indeed on the night before the ceremony the party went on into the small hours of the big day itself. At breakfast we were joined by John Rowley, the Controller of the BBC in Wales. I asked him; 'Did you sleep well?' He said, 'Well, the chap playing the piano under my room might have stopped sooner than he did.' We all realised that he knew I was the culprit, but to his credit no further mention was made of the matter.

My commentary position was at the top of the Chamberlain Tower, 150 feet above the ground, and after laboriously climbing the steps I was astounded to find two strangers there. They and I had each of us been assured that we would have the place exclusively to ourselves. They were plain clothes police officers, just a small part of the enormous security exercise, but a brief exchange in Welsh established acceptable credentials on all sides and indeed they provided me with very useful local material for the commentary.

On a fine day, from the Chamberlain Tower, you can see the summit of Snowdon, but she and her sister peaks were hidden in cloud that afternoon. Happily it was dry, although overcast, and the Union Jack and the Red Dragon of Wales fluttered high above the Eagle Tower in a stiff south-westerly breeze.

From early in the morning, the guests from all over the world had been arriving in Caernarfon. There were 4400 seats inside the castle and 2315 in the moat area. Those in the moat area had paid ten guineas for their seats and were given souvenir cushions in vermilion Welsh wool 'for their comfort at the ceremony and as a memento of the occasion'. The others were allowed, if they so wished, to buy the seats they occupied for twelve pounds, and I have since seen many of these scarlet chairs, with their gold Prince of Wales's feathers, taking pride of place in the best rooms of houses all over the world.

As I looked down from my position at the top of the tower, I remembered a previous royal occasion in 1953 when I stood on a slightly lower vantage point at Hyde Park's Stanhope Gate. Then, there were many hundreds below me who had camped out for several days and nights on the pavements lining the route of The Queen's Coronation procession. While the enthusiasm in 1969 did not quite equal that of the London crowds, the square outside the Castle was packed with people from a very early hour, and a party of American students had settled down with sleeping-bags on the pavement in the square at four o'clock the previous afternoon. They were the forerunners of many thousands of their compatriots who were to visit Caernarfon and its Castle in the years to come. There were several visitors from the USA in rather more comfortable circumstances inside the Castle, among them Patricia Nixon, the President's daughter, who sat near another American statesman who didn't make it to the White House, Hubert Humphrey.

As we waited for the ceremony, we listened to the music of the massed local choirs, the BBC Welsh Symphony Orchestra and a group of sixteen of Wales's greatest operatic and concert artistes. We heard the old traditional pennillion-singing of Wales and specially commissioned orchestral and choral works by contemporary composers of the Principality.

As preparation for my commentary I played a silent game of 'spot the celebrities' so that there would be some mental material standing by for use in the inevitable gaps in the proceedings. There was certainly no lack of celebrities, and it was fascinating to 'spot' among the waiting crowds people like the Maharajah and Maharanee of Jaipur, providing an exotic splash of oriental colour, and the Maharajah of Kupurtala, whose regiment in India is still called 'The Prince of Wales's Own.'

LEFT: *Alun Williams with a lip microphone (still used by commentators) on the top of the Chamberlain Tower at Caernarfon Castle, 150 feet above the ground.*

Among the Prince's personal guests were Michael Purse, his history master at the school he attended in Geelong, Australia; the former Headmaster of another of his old schools, Gordonstoun in Scotland; his senior tutor at Cambridge University, and two ladies who sat there very proudly – his former nannies Helen Lightbody and Mabel Anderson.

There were heralds, pursuivants of arms in ordinary and extra-ordinary, white-robed members of the Gorsedd of Bards, mayors of the boroughs and county boroughs, chairmen and clerks of the county councils, Her Majesty's High Sheriffs and those Welsh Members of Parliament who had agreed to attend, among whom was that colourful character Leo Abse, the Member for Pontypool, who always stole the sartorial limelight on Budget Day and who, for the Investiture, was adorned in a suit of gold with a polo-necked sweater.

There were lords, bishops and archbishops and representatives of the Free Churches – for this was a truly ecumenical gathering – and one very proud young Welsh schoolgirl, seventeen-year-old Margaret Helen Parry, daughter of a local non-conformist minister, who carried a very precious burden: the Bible of Bishop William Morgan whose Welsh translation in 1588 had, more than anything, been instrumental in preserving the Welsh language. She placed it on a special slate lectern from which we were soon to hear the readings of the Letters Patent.

For weeks beforehand all sections of the media had devoted much publicity to the political opposition to the ceremony and among many demonstrations and acts of protest, two Welshmen had been killed when a bomb they were carrying near the railway line a few miles from Caernarfon exploded. It was natural that those of us responsible for describing the proceedings were constantly mindful of this element, and we had been well briefed as to what we were to do should anything untoward happen.

I confess, therefore, that my heart stopped when we heard a sudden loud explosion – but all was well as Raymond Baxter from his commentary position in Caernarfon Square identified it as the first of a twenty-one gun salute fired on a hill across the River Seiont, which

*Twenty-year-old Prince Charles on his way to the Investiture at
Caernarfon Castle in a semi-state landau with
Mr George Thomas, Secretary of State for Wales,
and the Prince's Equerry, Sq. Ldr David Checketts.*

told us that the royal train had arrived at 'Griffiths crossing' by the
Menai Straits some two miles away and that The Queen was on her
way. The Prince had arrived there some ten minutes previously and
was on his way in the semi-state Landau drawn by four postillion-,
ridden bays, the carriage used by Queen Victoria at her Golden Jubilee
in 1887.

The Prince, in the uniform of Colonel-in-Chief of the Royal Regiment of Wales, arrived first with his Escort of forty troopers of the Life Guards and Blues and Royals, but for me the most important player in this part of the drama was the stud groom who preceded the Prince's procession on a Windsor Grey. He had to control the trotting speed of his mount to a nicety so that those behind him arrived at exactly the right moment. As the mounted troops and police slowed down to ride around the square, it was apparent that they needed all their strength to keep their sweating and foaming steeds properly under control.

Although Prince Charles was to be the leading player in the drama, protocol demanded that he remain in the wings until the arrival of his mother. He walked slowly along the Lower Ward of the Castle to the robing-room beneath the Chamberlain Tower to await her.

He was followed by the procession of Welsh youth of which I had heard in Sydney. There was J. P. R. Williams, the international rugby player, who had arrived from Fiji only twenty-four hours earlier; Edward Prichard from Anglesey, a boxer, Eisteddfod reciter and show-jumper; Wyn Griffin, a soccer player from Llandudno; Ian Thomas, a student at Oxford; Martin Woodruffe, whose swim for a silver medal at the Mexico Olympics the previous year I had described for BBC listeners; and many others representing various aspects of the life of youth in Wales.

Then we heard that The Queen's carriage was approaching, drawn by six Windsor Greys. She was accompanied by the Duke of Edinburgh in Field Marshal's uniform, and Princess Anne looking, in the words of a fashion expert, not 'as mod' as usual and wearing a turquoise blue 'button up' silk coat and a pill box hat with a cockade on the back. I was subsequently indebted to the same expert lady for the following details of the royal ladies' apparel:

THE QUEEN: a simple yellow parchment-coloured silk coat and a matching Tudor-style hat embroidered with small pearls. Her Majesty carried a matching umbrella and so had the distinction of being the only person present to carry one!

THE QUEEN MOTHER: an apple-green lace coat with flowing green organza and a large 'Breton' hat with five heron feathers tinted green.

PRINCESS MARGARET: a bright pink silk coat and a matching chiffon hat, in the words of my informant 'rather like a spaniel's ears'.

During our previous visit, Lord Snowdon had referred to several of the vermilion seats placed near the dais as 'flowerpot seats' and when the royal ladies reached them we realised why – their hats and colourful costumes added a splash of colour like little groups of flower pots on the green grass of the Castle's Upper Ward.

Lord Plunkett, the equerry-in-waiting, ascended the sixteen steps to the heavy oaken iron-studded door in the Water Gate, struck it firmly and called out,

'I demand admission in the name of The Queen!'

The bolts were drawn back and the Constable emerged from the darkness below the Tower carrying a cushion bearing the key, fifteen inches long.

'Madam, I surrender the key of this Castle into your Majesty's hands.'

The Queen replied, 'Sir Constable, I return the key of this Castle into your keeping.'

The Queen Mother and her following were already within, and the great crowd stood to receive her procession and that of The Queen, and when all had assembled on and around the dais, The Queen commanded the Earl Marshal (the Duke of Norfolk) to direct the Garter King of Arms (Sir Anthony Wagner) to summon His Royal Highness the Prince of Wales to her presence.

He walked towards the robing-room in his full dress uniform: a scarlet cloth coatee, its collar and cuffs of blue-black velvet heavily embroidered with gold thread on the front edges, and the collar, cuffs and pocket flaps lined with scarlet silk, and on his head a black beaver cocked hat with a black silk cockade and bordered with white ostrich feathers. My fashion expert was very impressed by the uniforms of the men and readily admitted that, for once, they outshone the women!

The Prince then approached his mother. He was preceded by the Wales and Chester Heralds of Arms and behind him came Lord Davies, Lord Dynevor, the Earl Lloyd George of Dwyfor bearing the sword, (from the Middle Ages, earls and upwards have been invested with a sword, and it signified that the Prince had also been created Earl of Chester); Lord Ogmore with the crown (very much a twentieth-century streamlined version, weighing only three pounds, worth about £24 000 with seventy-five diamonds and twelve emeralds and a cap of state of purple velvet inside); Lord Maelor with the gold ring (signifying the marriage of the Prince to the Principality – a single smooth amethyst held by two interlaced Welsh dragons, their heads and claws forming a setting for the stones); Lord Heycock with the golden rod (at its head three winged cherubs supporting the Prince's crown); and Lord Harlech with the mantle. This was similar in design to the great cloak worn by his great uncle Edward at the last Investiture in 1911 but without the flowing train. It had an ermine collar with black dots, the Prince of Wales's feathers on the edging and a clasp of eighteen carat gold. The Home Secretary, James Callaghan, then stood at the slate lectern and read the Letters Patent.

'Elizabeth the Second, by the Grace of God, of the United Kingdom of Great Britain and Northern Ireland and of our other realms and territories – Head of the Commonwealth, Defender of the Faith. To all our Lords Spiritual and Temporal and all our other subjects whatsoever to whom these presents shall come, greetings. Know ye, that we have made and created and by these our letters do make and create our most dear son, Charles Philip Arthur George, Prince of the United Kingdom of Great Britain and Northern Ireland, Duke of Cornwall and Rothesay, Earl of Carrick, Baron of Renfrew, Lord of the Isles and Great Steward of Scotland, Prince of Wales and Earl of Chester; and to the same our most dear son, Charles Philip Arthur George have given and granted and by this our present Charter do give, grant and confer the name, style, title, dignity and honour of the same Principality and Earldom; and him, our most dear son, Charles Philip Arthur George, as has been accustomed, we do ennoble and invest with the said Principality and Earldom by girting him with

The Prince of Wales kneels before his mother and is invested with the sword, crown, rod, ring and mantle.

a sword, by putting a coronet on his head and a gold ring on his finger and also by delivering a gold rod into his hand that he may preside there and may direct and defend those parts, to hold to him and his heirs, Kings of the United Kingdom of Great Britain and Northern Ireland, and of our other realms and territories, Heads of the Commonwealth, for ever.

'Wherefore we will and strictly command for us, our heirs and successors, that our most dear son Charles Philip Arthur George may have the name, style, title, state, dignity and honour of the Principality of Wales and Earldom of Chester aforesaid unto him and his heirs, Kings of the United Kingdom of Great Britain and Northern Ireland and of our other realms and territories, Heads of the Commonwealth as is above mentioned; in witness whereof we have caused these our Letters to be made Patent. Witness ourself, at Westminster, the twenty-sixth day of July in the seventh year of our reign.'

These Letters Patent were then read in Welsh by George Thomas, the Secretary of State for Wales, who had ridden to Caernarfon in the Prince's carriage. The man later to become Speaker of the House of Commons and Viscount Tonypandy, although not a Welsh speaker, had obviously prepared his pronunciations very carefully indeed! As he read the Welsh version the Prince, kneeling bareheaded before his mother, was invested by her with the sword, crown, rod, ring and mantle. He looked up at her with a faint smile and when the reading had finished he did homage for the Principality by placing his hands in an attitude of prayer between those of The Queen.

'I, Charles, Prince of Wales, do become your liege man of life and limb and earthly worship; and faith and truth I will bear unto thee, to live and die against all manner of folk.' The Queen kissed her son on the cheek – the kiss of fealty, the pledge that the overlord, The Queen, would henceforth protect the vassal, the Prince.

Then more fanfares. Colonel Jaeger, the Director of Music, with his five bands and various trumpeters around the battlements, can never have directed a more scattered ensemble. The groups, some of them nearly a hundred yards away, were at various points in a great semi-circle around the walls of the Castle; he must have felt that to be conducting in the Hollywood Bowl would be child's play!

In his response to The Loyal Address by the President of Aberystwyth University, Sir Ben Bowen Thomas, the newly invested Prince again revealed that his two-month stay at that college had indeed been fruitful. He spoke in Welsh and English and his delivery in the ancient language was superb. He, like George Thomas, had obviously burned

*The Prince of Wales is presented to the Welsh people
at Queen Eleanor's Gate. The last time this had occurred
was in 1911 when his great uncle, Edward VIII
was presented to the people.*

the midnight oil, although he confessed to me many years later that by then, to his great regret, much of what he had learned at Aberystwyth had been forgotten.

Then, in the religious service that followed, we sang the old Welsh hymn tunes, and they had never sounded quite like this, with a great chorus, a full symphony orchestra and the thousands outside joining in.

King Edward I promised the Welsh people that he would present to them a prince who spoke no English. He was as good as his word, for the son of Queen Eleanor of Castile was a babe-in-arms. In 1911 from the Castle gate overlooking the square which was named after that same Eleanor, the Prince who was never to be crowned as King Edward VIII was presented to the Welsh people, and on this day in 1969 this tradition of the centuries was once again honoured.

The great crowds, cheerfully unmindful of the slight drizzle of rain now falling, roared their welcome as Charles stood between his parents and the shouts rose to a great crescendo as The Queen linked her hand with her son's and held it on high.

The Procession of State then returned along the Lower Ward and here we saw a touching family interlude as the Prince and his parents approached The Queen Mother, Princess Anne and Princess Margaret. (I was so overcome with emotion that I referred to them as his grandmother and two sisters!) His Aunt Margaret started to applaud and the rest joined in. Then to the King's Gate for the second presentation to the people and finally back to the Water Gate and the waiting carriage. As twelve Phantom aircraft of the Royal Air Force flew low overhead in aerial salute, the rain stopped and the sun came out.

In his response to The Loyal Address, Prince Charles said of Wales,

'What a Principality!'

We who were there still say,

'What a Prince! What an Investiture!'

THE INVESTITURE OF HIS ROYAL HIGHNESS THE PRINCE OF WALES – A DESIGNER'S VIEW

THE EARL OF SNOWDON

The designer's view of an event is very different from that of the broadcaster. The commentator usually arrives when all the preparations are complete, while the designer has to be there when the first plans are formulated.

The designer for the Investiture of the Prince of Wales was the Constable of Caernarfon Castle and uncle of Prince Charles, Lord Snowdon. The spectacular ceremony was just two hours long, but it succeeded in stirring emotions right across the world and gave a massive boost to the Welsh tourist economy. This was all very gratifying to Lord Snowdon for he had spent the previous two years designing the event, as he explains.

I FIRST BECAME INVOLVED in the Investiture plans in 1964, when Her Majesty asked me to be Constable of Caernarfon Castle. It was general knowledge that Prince Charles would be invested there one day, but no one knew when. As Constable, I was responsible for preparing the Castle for the ceremony, so from that time on everyone thought I knew the date and was being terribly discreet. Actually I was in the dark, too.

Ignorance notwithstanding, I was extremely honoured to be given the job. I am Welsh, and being Welsh means a lot to me. I grew up in North Wales, three miles from Caernarfon, and I thought that this would be an opportunity to do something for Wales. I knew that the Investiture would be televised, and this would be a chance to put Caernarfon on the map. The important thing was that the occasion was good for Wales and the Welsh, not just for the people who believed in the monarchy but for everyone, whatever their political views might be.

I used the next three years to carry out a general cleaning up process at the Castle. It was in a poor state: there were very obtrusive railings on the ramparts and signs everywhere saying 'Toilets', and there were awful little paths carving up the grass courtyards. I decided that we should return the Castle to basics and let it speak for itself in the simplest possible way. That would be very effective for the Investiture itself and it would be good for the Castle in the long run.

In 1967, the date of the Investiture was set for 1 July 1969. All kinds of things were taken into consideration when they chose that day. It hadn't to clash with the Welsh Agricultural Fair and with the various Eisteddfods. It should be during school-term time so that the people of Wales were at home, rather than off on holiday, but ideally the university term should be over so that the university hostels at Bangor could be used for accommodation if necessary. So 1 July was chosen and the Earl Marshal, the Duke of Norfolk, was appointed to take charge of the arrangements. He then asked me if I would be in charge of the design of the ceremony.

I was on the main committee with the Duke of Norfolk, the Ministry of Public Buildings and Works, Members of Parliament, the

Lord Snowdon, Constable of Caernarfon Castle, arrives for a full dress rehearsal of the Investiture ceremony. He was regarded as a 'sixties whizz kid'.

Wales Tourist Board and all sorts of other people. I immediately suggested that we form a design sub-committee and I asked one of my greatest friends, Carl Toms the theatre designer – who had been my uncle Oliver Messel's assistant – if he'd come and work on it. He agreed, and I was also given John Pound from the Ministry of Works, along with an excellent engineer from the Ministry called Bob Hancock. Carl and John were complete opposites but despite that, or because of it, they worked very well together. The Duke of Norfolk was a wonderful organiser. At first I thought I hadn't much in common with him, but I ended by admiring him totally. He was meticulous, efficient, very lovable and whenever a design problem arose he'd say, 'Oh you go ahead and get on with it, do what you want.'

Carl and I shared the same ideas about simplicity. We saw that if we kept things very simple, the architectural grandeur of the Castle would benefit. We wanted as little decoration as possible, just to emphasise the green of the grass and the grey of the Castle walls, to let the whole thing be as it would have been in the time of Henry V. But we were also very aware that we were designing the ceremony for television, and that it was to be televised in colour, which was quite new then. So we were thinking continually about where the cameras were going to be, and it was vitally important that things weren't artificially lit. The logistics of television influenced all our ideas and I think it was the first ceremony of that kind to be designed for the people at home. I wanted television viewers to feel that they were actually there.

It was to be a great spectacle, with the utmost simplicity and elegance. Television would have a viewing of millions (it was 500 million in the end), and I wanted it to appeal to all kinds of people, whatever their politics. I wanted it to be entirely Welsh too, with everything made from Welsh materials.

We scribbled down sketches and notes. We went back to 1911, when the last Investiture took place, to see what they had done. In fact, though there have been Princes of Wales since the fourteenth century (Edward II was the first), the 1911 Investiture was the first one to take place in Wales. That was in Caernarfon too, in a small green and white striped tent. Even the small élite that had been asked inside the Castle could see little of it; the public saw nothing.

At the beginning there were meetings in St James's Palace, around a huge table. I think I was regarded as a sixties whizz kid; really very *mal vu*, and so when I said that I'd thought of making the canopy over the central dais in perspex, so that cameras could film the proceedings from any angle they wished, there were various dignitaries who said, 'Plastic? Good God! There must be a canopy at the entrance. You can't see the monarch going up steps! It's never been done before. The people just have to see her going straight onto the red carpet, and then under a canopy until she appears on the dais.'

I said, 'There's not going to be a red carpet.'

'What do you mean, there's not going to be a red carpet? What about all that grass?'

I said, 'Well it seems to me that if you're designing a theatrical event, you tell the main characters that they're going to be walking on grass and they wear the right shoes.'

Okay. Hurdle number one (reluctantly) cleared. No canopy over the entrance, and a small one in perspex over the central dais.

At another meeting, Carl and I showed designs for banners to hang on the walls. Carl had made the drawings of the banners very elegant, very traditional; some would have coats of arms on them, some would have the red dragon. Carl and I designed a dragon specially for one of the banners: it was a very simple Welsh dragon, without flourishes. 'Yes but look here,' someone objected as the design was passed round, 'whoever's seen a dragon without a knot in its tail?'

So it went on. We wanted a slate dais because slate was a Welsh material and it also had an austere quality which we liked. We designed a very plain, circular slate dais in the centre, with steps leading round it, completely surrounded by grass. Carl and I then worked out that we'd have just four stainless steel poles supporting the curved perspex canopy which would focus attention and, if necessary, keep off a little bit of rain. The canopy also lent some grandeur to the dais because it had the Prince of Wales's feathers on it, moulded in expanded polystyrene and gilded. It sounds awful when I describe it like that, but in fact it looked very good both in reality and on television.

The Prince of Wales's feathers I had found on a belt plate belonging to the Cader Idris Infantry Volunteers, dating from about 1805. The right-hand feather bent backwards which made the whole design less formal and more romantic.

How would conventional ornate gilt thrones tune in with the starkness of the slate dais? We did not think that they would, so we designed the thrones out of simple plain slabs of slate held together with stainless steel bolts. Only the central one for Her Majesty had a back which gave it more visual importance and added height. The other two were simple stools with arms – all had vermilion cushions made of Welsh wool. It was, of course, all discussed beforehand and exact measurements were made for the correct height. Not having backs to the thrones was a great benefit to the cameras.

The budget we had was a small one, quite rightly, otherwise it would have been criticised as an extravaganza: £55 000 (to include scaffolding and building work) was a tight squeeze even in 1969. I believed from the outset that the tax-payers should not have to foot the bill, especially as there were some people in Wales who disapproved of the whole thing. But it meant that we had to be ingenious about getting materials cheap or free. We used every contact we had, asked suppliers for discounts, requested donations from the BBC and ITA.

The slates for the dais and thrones were donated by the Port Dinorwic slate quarry, owned by my godfather Sir Michael Duff. The canopies were made by what was then the British Aircraft Corporation at a discount; the company which made the Prince of Wales's feathers motifs did so at a loss; the music stands for the orchestra we didn't buy at all but borrowed; and so it went on.

With over 4000 guests to be accommodated inside the Castle, seating was obviously going to be one of our major expenses. So we decided to sell the chairs as souvenirs.

The Ministry of Works wanted the VIP chairs to be very ornate (costing fifty pounds), while the 'riff-raff' – the other 4000 people – would just sit on scaffolding. Our views didn't agree with that. Instead I proposed that everyone had the same chair, a very simple design of

Lord Snowdon's design was influenced by the logistics of television. A striking element was the chairs which were stained vermilion to contrast with the grey castle and the green grass. They were all sold after the event.

laminated ply made in Wales, stained vermilion and with a seat of Welsh tweed and the Prince of Wales's feathers in gold on the back. The only difference would be that the VIPs' chairs had arms and legs and the others just screwed onto the scaffolding. If anyone wanted to buy one as a souvenir, they would get the whole thing delivered in a box – seat and frame with four screws to assemble it – for twelve pounds, including packing and postage.

At the beginning of the day it was terrifying because the only ones which had sold were the six I had bought, but by the end they'd sold out. We also made cushions for members of the public outside the Castle who were to sit in the moat areas. These were vermilion wool trimmed with a gold lurex rope, and they too went on sale, at thirty-five shillings each. After the ceremony, there was such a demand for them that a batch of extras was made to fill the orders.

There were many other things that we were doing to make Caernarfon Castle better for the public. I was anxious to improve the quality of souvenirs and so I initiated a scheme with the Design Council to offer an award for the best designed souvenirs – from the very cheapest things like pencils, to more expensive items. At the top end of the scale I asked John Piper if he'd do some drawings of the Castle, and Carl Toms and I designed a mug for Wedgwood.

We also published a new brochure for the Castle, and together with John Pound I redesigned the Castle shop in slate, stainless steel and glass. There was another empty room in the Castle which I decorated, and I managed to borrow some armour from the Tower of London and put it on display in slate and glass cases. We had to take care that the cases were watertight, because it's very windy in the castle and very damp. It was important to get the Castle looking as good as possible for the Investiture, and these would be beneficial long-term improvements too.

All this time, we had people working on the fabric of the Castle and the layout, so that we had as large and plain an area of grass as possible. In February 1969, the Castle was closed and the full-scale preparations began. Much of the present Castle was built and dolled up in 1911, and ever since then people have been having a go at 'improving' it. Charming, generous people had lent this and lent that – there were even two Spanish bronze cannons there – and so I was busy trying to get rid of things without hurting people's feelings. I usually said (and it was conveniently true) that they were getting very damp in Caernarfon and would be better off somewhere else. Gradually, I shifted out the clutter and restored the rooms to their rightful emptiness and simplicity.

At this stage I was having regular meetings with Antony Craxton of the BBC and various people from ITV to find out what the ideal requirements for television were. I wanted them to be able to film the whole ceremony – especially the principal participants, Her Majesty

The Queen, Prince Philip and Prince Charles – from all possible angles, as well as the choir, orchestra and general vistas of the entire scene. But I didn't want there to be any cameras in view of another camera. When you were watching in your sitting-room at home, you wouldn't be aware of the media being there. Therefore cameras could not be fixed on the parapets; instead I suggested they were mounted on hoists, so that they could extend upwards to take a rooftop shot and then go back down below the castellations immediately afterwards.

The more we looked into the technicalities of the broadcast, the more problems we discovered. For instance, at the end of the ceremony Her Majesty The Queen would present Prince Charles to the people at Queen Eleanor's Gate. The gate was to be decorated with motifs and banners and there would be four trumpeters on the roof who would announce the presentation. But they would have to have their backs to the camera in order to see the conductor on the inside. We wanted a camera outside in the square to focus on the trumpeters playing and then come down onto The Queen and Prince Charles below.

'Well it's hard luck, you can't do it, as they must see me,' said the conductor.

'It's a very short tune,' I protested, 'Can't they learn it?' But he insisted that the trumpeters needed to see him, so in the end I arranged for a second conductor with a walkie-talkie to go on the roof of Caernarfon post office, on the other side of the square, and the trumpeters took their lead from him.

I was trying to design the ceremony partly as a photographer, partly as a documentary film maker and partly as the nephew of my uncle Oliver Messel, the theatre designer. It was after all a theatrical production, designed for the enjoyment of as many people as possible.

For the last few months before the Investiture, we (Carl, John, Bob Hancock and I) lived on a boat which had kindly been lent to us. My home was only a few miles away but it was easier to live on the boat moored alongside the Castle. I had a speedboat there as well, which provided us with an alternative means of transport if the roads were blocked. By now, preparations for the Investiture were attracting more people to Caernarfon.

We were out one evening in a small boat (going for a barbecue) when suddenly we heard a large bang and an enormous splash exploded just near us. I swerved in to Bellan Fort and we saw a number of people there, apparently at a cocktail party. There was quite a bit of smoke around, and it turned out that Lord Newborough had just let off one of his cannons across the Menai Straits from his Napoleonic fort. I changed direction and moored in his harbour and said to him, 'You could have sunk us!'

'Well, how did I know it was you?' he said indignantly. The man in charge of the Harbour Trust smiled.

'Oh what a pity you didn't sink,' he observed.

'Why?' I asked.

'It would have been such an honour for our lads to have come and rescued you, you see.'

The best view of Caernarfon Castle is from the Menai Straits and I had a wild idea to try to get permission to have the royal yacht moored just in front of the Castle. Unfortunately I discovered that at low tide it would only have a clearance of three inches when it was dead calm. So, sadly that was a non-starter.

With about a month to go, Carl and I took Prince Charles to the Castle to see how the ceremony would work. It was a very quiet visit; no one knew about it except my father's boatman, a marvellous man called Evan Lloyd. We went out in his fishing boat so we could get the best view of the Castle (where the yacht was intended to be). We then roughly walked through the ceremony, showing His Royal Highness sketches and models so he could get the gist of what it would be like on the day.

The perspex canopy for the dais arrived, complete in one sculpted piece. It looked excellent but it seemed exactly the width of the main gate. How on earth were we to get it in? We thought of hoisting it over the walls with a crane, or flying it in by helicopter, but there are terrific winds on that coast and there was too great a danger of the canopy breaking. Eventually we manoeuvred it at an angle through the main gate with two inches to spare.

We also had a dark green canopy set up for the orchestra, placing it against the wall so it didn't detract from the central dais. Ideally I hadn't wanted a second canopy, but it was necessary to protect their strings in case of rain. The matter of canopies and rain cover had been a bone of contention from the start: various people on the committees had wanted a cover for the VIPs but I had said no. 'But what's going to happen if it rains?' they asked. 'It'll be just like the Duke of Norfolk said about the Coronation,' I replied; 'we'll all get bloody wet.'

The colours of the Castle were emerging now. The grass had been nursed by the Castle gardeners over the last few months and it was lush and green. Against it the dark slate dais, steps and lectern looked dramatic, but in keeping with the Castle itself. The banners, predominantly white and scarlet, had been delivered, but of course we couldn't put them out yet.

It was very exciting seeing it come together, but there were a lot of last minute anxieties. It's such a nightmare, suddenly realising at that stage that you've left something out. Most of the hitches were very small but we did have one large problem with sight-lines. Because of a jutting-out internal structure, people sitting on the north side in Lower Ward wouldn't be able to see a thing of the ceremony. It was all very well saying that we were designing it for television, but it was too much to leave all these lord mayors and so on without even a squint of the dais. We had six eight-feet by four-feet looking-glasses made of plastic and hung them on the walls opposite. But I'd been an absolute fool and had not realised that, however large a piece of looking-glass is and however you angle it, it only reflects a very small area, so it would have worked for about eight seats only. The answer, I realised belatedly, was to have convex plastic looking-glasses about five feet in diameter which gave everyone a wide-angle view. We got the trumpeters to blow them up. It worked quite well and if they were televised they weren't noticeable, but I was worried that, being plastic, the looking-glasses could burst. If a seagull flew into one, for instance, it would probably rip. So as a safeguard I had some small television sets, screens specially shaded, set against the south wall, high enough not to be in shot.

I went up to London for a rehearsal in the garden of Buckingham

Palace. It wasn't a rehearsal in the conventional sense because the main characters were not present, but we had some able stand-ins. The Garter King of Arms, Sir Anthony Wagner, was one. He was dressed in a bowler hat and a mackintosh and carried an umbrella for the mace. Then there was somebody else, I can't remember who, as Prince Charles. He wore a terrible little crown from Nathan's or some other costumiers. The whole thing was worked out with bits of string representing steps as the lawn is totally flat. It was lovely, all these people dressed in raincoats and holding umbrellas, going up imaginary steps. The choirs and orchestra were having their own rehearsals in the meantime, and so were the members of the various processions.

The order of events was that once all the guests and choirs and so forth were in the Castle, Prince Charles would arrive by carriage. He would go into the Chamberlain Tower, where we had made a robing room for him. Then Her Majesty The Queen and Prince Philip would arrive, also by carriage, and as Constable of the Castle I would perform the Ceremony of the Keys, admitting her at the Water Gate entrance. I was rather keen that the carriages came down the hill, past the southern façade and up to Water Gate that way, because it would look marvellous on television, with the south side of the Castle as a backdrop. But it was vetoed because the hill is extremely steep and the brakes wouldn't have been able to hold the carriages.

The evening before the Investiture, everything in the Castle was ready, and safely covered up from the weather. I didn't stay on the boat that night: Carl and I went back to my home.

We got up at dawn and went to the Castle, where we supervised a team of about thirty people tearing off all the polystyrene covers from the seats. It was a marvellous sight: the lush green grass, the white and scarlet banners, the grey of the Castle walls and the dais, and most exciting of all, the mass of scarlet chairs. The emptiness of it gave it an added impact.

After that stunning moment, I spent the next few hours whizzing round checking details, conferring with the television crews, searching the grass for stray cigarette butts. I prayed it wouldn't rain.

I had a part to play as Constable of the Castle, so I changed into

Lord Snowdon, wearing what was described in the newspapers as a 'Buttons' outfit'. As Constable of the Castle, he performed the Ceremony of the Keys.

a special uniform Carl had designed for me. It provoked some mirth in the papers the next day – it was described as a 'Buttons' outfit, although actually it had no buttons at all. It was a dark green tailcoat with no decorative bits, no gold braid, no hat, just a black sash and an Indian-type collar with the Prince of Wales's feathers on either side. It was kept as simple and functional as possible. But in retrospect I think it was rather silly.

Prince Charles arrived and went to the Chamberlain Tower, from which he would later emerge to take part in the ceremony. Then The Queen's carriage arrived and I had to go down and open the gate. I had this huge key – it was a fake, made in 1911 – and at the last moment someone produced a terrible maroon velvet tray with a string round it, which I was supposed to wear round my neck. I felt just like a cinema usherette selling ice-cream, so I objected rather firmly and said that I preferred just to carry the key.

The procedure is known as the Ceremony of the Keys and it actually worked well as a piece of theatre. There was a great banging on the door by Lord Plunkett, Equerry and Deputy Master of the Household. He demanded admission in the name of The Queen and, after a pause and some stage rattling for sound effects, I unlocked the gates. As Her Majesty came up the steps I took the key to her and said, 'Madam, I surrender the key of this Castle into Your Majesty's hand.' The Queen touched the key and replied, 'Sir Constable, I return the key of this Castle into your keeping.' Then I handed the key over to the Head Custodian and took The Queen into the Castle. After that I took my place in a line of chairs, just to one side of the dais, and became a spectator.

Today, my memories of the Investiture itself are fragmented. I remember the music being glorious – they had Huw Wheldon and Geraint Evans giving invaluable advice. The rain held off: it just drizzled at one point and even then only one person, who shall be nameless, put on a mackintosh. I remember wishing that I had been able to influence the clothes worn by the main characters. I should have liked to see The Queen and Queen Elizabeth The Queen Mother in Garter gowns – long gowns down to the ground – rather than day

*King George VI and Queen Elizabeth listen to their new
portable wireless in 1948 – the year of their silver wedding.*

The Imperial State Crown on its way from Buckingham Palace to the Palace of Westminster for the State Opening of Parliament.

*Her Majesty The Queen processes through the Royal Gallery
to the chamber of the House of Lords during the State Opening
of Parliament.*

TOP: *More than a million poppy petals float down from the ceiling of the Royal Albert Hall at the close of the Festival of Remembrance.*

ABOVE: *King Olav V of Norway, The Princess of Wales, The Princess Royal, Princess Alice, Duchess of Gloucester and The Queen Mother watch the service of Remembrance at the Cenotaph.*

Her Majesty The Queen receiving flowers from children during
a walkabout after the Royal Maundy Service held at Worcester
Cathedral in 1980.

TOP: *The Sovereign's Escort of the Household Cavalry prepare to walk past Her Majesty The Queen during the Trooping the Colour ceremony.*

ABOVE: *Her Majesty The Queen rides back to Buckingham Palace after a wet Trooping the Colour ceremony in 1982.*

The Queen Mother holding hands with her grandson, The Prince of Wales, at the close of the Garter Day ceremony at Windsor.

TOP: *The Queen presents The Prince of Wales to the crowds outside Caernarfon Castle after the Investiture in 1969.*

ABOVE: *Her Majesty The Queen and The Duke of Edinburgh at the close of the Thanksgiving service held in St Paul's Cathedral to celebrate the Silver Jubilee in 1977.*

TOP: *On the eve of the wedding of Prince Charles and Lady Diana Spencer a fireworks display was held in London's Hyde Park, watched by a crowd of over half a million.*

ABOVE: *Her Majesty The Queen with the Dean of Windsor and members of the Royal Family on the steps of St George's Chapel, Windsor after the Christmas Day service in 1980.*

*A camera-eye view of the interior of St Paul's Cathedral
during the wedding of Prince Charles and Lady Diana Spencer.*

TOP: *The bridesmaids enter St Paul's Cathedral for the wedding of Prince Charles to Lady Diana Spencer, 29 July 1981. The chief bridesmaid was Lady Sarah Armstrong-Jones.*

ABOVE: *The Prince and Princess of Wales leave Buckingham Palace for Waterloo station at the beginning of their honeymoon.*

The Prince and Princess of Wales on a visit to Australia
during the bicentenary celebrations in 1988.

Her Majesty The Queen has just been given a bouquet by the grandson of the Governor of Canton Province during her tour of China in 1986.

*The Princess of Wales receives garlands in Hong Kong during
a royal tour of the Far East in 1989.*

*The Duke and Duchess of York after their marriage at
Westminster Abbey, 23 July 1986. The Duke of York wore
the uniform of a naval lieutenant.*

TOP: *The Queen Mother, The Princess Margaret and Lady Sarah Armstrong-Jones watching the Badminton Horse Trials in 1973.*

ABOVE: *The Queen Mother re-visits the East End of London and meets local people during the celebrations for her 90th birthday.*

dresses. I thought Prince Charles's scarlet robes looked splendid, but I'd have preferred a simpler crown, just a band of gold rather than something with spikes. Mostly, the ceremony is a series of scenes imprinted on my mind: Prince Charles on the dais, the slate thrones beneath the canopy, the trumpeters on the parapets announcing the appearance of The Queen and Prince Charles on the balcony below.

The ceremony lasted about two hours. Afterwards I took Prince Charles to the Chamberlain Tower which I'd had glazed and which had served as a robing room. I had designed a simple pine table for it, and on the walls hung plastic looking glasses, put in there to lighten up the room because the windows were tiny. There were eight Investiture chairs and it was lit with those round Japanese paper lamps. Rush matting was on the floor. The whole thing was very much of the sixties, and it's still there today: the public can look in through a perspex door to see it exactly as it was. Before he left, Prince Charles signed the table in pencil, which I thought would soon fade, so later we had it engraved on a stainless steel square, inlaid into the table top.

We had a party on the boat that night. I was so relieved that everything had gone without a hitch; it was one of the most exciting things I've ever done and I was very honoured to be asked to contribute to it. I think that if you asked the majority of Welsh people, they would say it was well worthwhile, not just for that memorable day but, in the long term, for Wales. Five hundred million people around the world saw the Investiture on television and it gave a great boost to Welsh tourism. The Castle gained from all the improvements: the slate dais is still there and is quite often used for theatrical occasions and military displays. Now, I'm happy to say, Caernarfon Castle gets more visitors than anywhere else in Wales.

And we did, in fact, manage to sell all the chairs as souvenirs.

THE
SILVER JUBILEE
– A PERSONAL
ACCOUNT

ROBERT HUDSON

Robert Hudson had been a freelance broadcaster for two years when he was asked to commentate at the service in St Paul's Cathedral, London for the Silver Jubilee of Her Majesty Queen Elizabeth II. He had an unusual mix of experience because his career at the BBC had included administration, management, production and microphone work. He knew what it was like to commentate at and organise big events for radio. Several years before, when he was Head of Outside Broadcasts for BBC Radio, Robert Hudson had been responsible for planning their coverage of the Investiture of His Royal Highness The Prince of Wales.

The Silver Jubilee year of 1977 was crowded with celebrations, but the service at St Paul's Cathedral was the main event and he had 'the best view in the house' – the commentary box.

A T 8.00 A.M. ON SUNDAY 5 JUNE 1977, I found myself standing at Temple Bar beside the Gold State Coach. It was empty. Two days later, at the more civilised hour of 11.15, Her Majesty The Queen would lean from its open door to touch the Pearl Sword, an historic symbol of her Sovereignty, proffered by the Lord Mayor of London.

The eight Windsor Greys would then draw this fairy-tale vehicle, refurbished and in use for the first time since the Coronation, up Ludgate Hill to St Paul's Cathedral in exactly twelve minutes. Today was the rehearsal; Tuesday would be the Silver Jubilee.

It was to be a busy week. My seventeenth assignation with Trooping the Colour, on Horse Guards Parade, would take place on the Saturday and the Garter Ceremony, at St George's Chapel, Windsor, on the following Monday; a 'hat-trick' of major royal broadcasts in six days. So much pomp and circumstance had attracted the attention of BBC Radio London, anxious to find out if it would damage my health. Accordingly my every step was dogged by the affable Roger Clark, armed with a tape recorder, to measure my ceremonial indigestion for a special programme. Indeed, facts, figures and timings were filling my notebooks at an alarming rate and I had heard enough fanfares and military music to last a lifetime.

As I walked up Ludgate Hill, stopwatch in hand, it soon became clear that the Gold Coach, its rubber tyres making a swishing noise on the wet road, was, so to speak, exceeding the speed limit. Indeed, it arrived at St Paul's in ten and a quarter minutes instead of the scheduled twelve; a quick check with the coachman confirmed that a brisk pace must be maintained to pull the heavy coach up the hill. So would it take the same time on Tuesday? It would. This was to prove useful information.

In 1977, I already had thirty years' broadcasting experience behind me. Two years earlier, I had retired from my job as Head of BBC Radio Outside Broadcasts Department to concentrate on lecturing, freelance broadcasting and in helping my wife with her antiques business. My thoughts turned to what I would have been doing had I still been in my executive chair, immersed in financial planning and contractual problems, in the siting of outside broadcast points and in the difficult decision of who would do what, and where, on the great day.

Although my workload at the microphone would be heavy, I knew how to tackle each broadcast, was confident of success and never lost a wink of sleep. The prerequisites of a commentator are talent, opportunity, experience and time to prepare. Given these, microphone work is a pleasure. In contrast, those behind the scenes are beset with intractable problems, in solving which they get little thanks and certainly no public recognition.

So it was with a light heart that I trudged up Ludgate Hill.

My perch two days later was to be in the west gallery of St Paul's, my task to set the scene inside and to lead radio listeners through the Thanksgiving Service. So why was I bothering with the carriage procession if I was not going to describe it? Quite simply, because knowledge breeds confidence. Much of what I had gleaned would be superfluous, but no matter. I now had forty-eight hours to decide how best to blend what was important and interesting with the magic of a very special royal occasion – and to do it at exactly the right place and in precisely the time available; a juggling act with words and seconds.

The Silver Jubilee was, in reality, three months of national celebration, from early May to the end of July, with 7 June as the focal point. Street parties, 2500 of them on Merseyside alone, fireworks and bonfires were to be the backcloth for the royal progress from Buckingham Palace to St Paul's and, after the service, on foot to a civic luncheon at the Guildhall.

It was only the second Silver Jubilee to be celebrated by any monarch – and, incidentally, the first to have a commentator inside St Paul's to describe it – so I was to make a little bit of history myself. Queen Victoria, in mourning for Prince Albert, preferred to await first the fifty-year milestone, and then her Diamond Jubilee in 1897. At the age of seventy-eight, the steps leading up to St Paul's were deemed too daunting an obstacle and the service was held outside as she sat in her carriage. In contrast The Queen Mother found no such difficulty in 1980 when celebrating her eightieth birthday at St Paul's!

A glance at the royal diary from May to July 1977 compels

admiration for the endurance and stamina of The Queen and Prince Philip. The schedule included major visits to Scotland before Jubilee Day, and to Wales, Northern Ireland and virtually every corner of England after it. Add to that, reviews of the Royal Navy, the Army, the Royal Air Force and the Police, as well as celebratory concerts, performances and exhibitions of every conceivable kind, and one appreciates how important the adulation of the nation must have been to help them on their way.

I had not been idle either. A two-hour LP called *Vivat Regina*, and special programmes about The Queen for the World Service, had kept me busy. I certainly felt well briefed.

Pageantry reflects our way of life and the British have a flair for organising it, unmatched anywhere else in the world. It is based on the oldest hereditary monarchy, the love of which, by the vast majority of people, has saved us from revolution. Similarly the English Channel has saved us from invasion for over 900 years, a point which the builders of the Channel Tunnel might like to note! So our rich heritage has survived, based on the Sovereign, the Church and Parliament.

The Silver Jubilee of Queen Elizabeth II had the trappings of a state occasion and most people would have said it was one. In fact, it was not; it was a royal occasion. Missing were some of the ingredients which, for example, make the State Opening of Parliament our only annual state occasion in the true sense. The Queen did not wear a crown nor the Robe of State, but rather a dress and coat of pink silk with a matching hat trimmed with twenty-five bell-shaped tassels. The Pearl Sword of the City of London, not the Sword of State, was carried before her in procession and the organisation was in the hands of the Lord Chamberlain, the Head of The Queen's Household, and not of the Earl Marshal, the Duke of Norfolk, who is responsible for state occasions.

All ceremonial has its roots in the past and, for the student of pageantry, the Silver Jubilee was a valuable exercise, as the present-day holders of strange titles, wearing gorgeous and exotic uniforms, took up their symbolic positions near the Sovereign. At the top of the steps of St Paul's, for all the world like court playing-cards come to life, in their tabards of scarlet, blue and gold, stood the Heralds and Pursuivants. They would precede The Queen in procession, as they did centuries ago, as the Sovereign's messengers and the organisers of the great tournaments of those days. Occasionally one would blow his nose to prove he was real.

Inside, at the east end of the nave, we find the Yeomen of the Guard, raised by Henry VII after the Battle of Bosworth in 1485, and selected from his 'private guard of faithful fellowes'. They still look the part today in their scarlet and gold tunics, with the history of the English Crown – the Tudor rose, the thistle and the shamrock – literally woven into them. Their Colour bears the Red Dragon of Wales. They are the oldest of The Queen's Bodyguards, but the honour of standing nearest to The Queen goes to the gentlemen-at-arms, raised by Henry VIII when he came to the throne in 1509, as 'a new and sumptuous Troop of Gentlemen'. They will stand beneath the dome of St Paul's, wearing their helmets even in church, with distinctive white feathers protruding from them. Their coats are red with blue velvet cuffs, white gloves, gold belts and epaulettes. The distinguished ex-officers, who form this élite corps, make a splendid sight.

To the man and woman in the street – and there must have been a million in London – the historical meaning of the pageantry in St Paul's would probably be lost – but it would look marvellous in colour on the 'telly'. The royal procession from Buckingham Palace would afford a more practical and visible example. Most people would recognise the Household Cavalry, the Life Guards in front in red tunics with the Blues and Royals behind the Gold Coach, but would they know that they fought on opposite sides in the Civil War and that they had yielded precedence as 'Right of the Line' to the King's Troop Royal Horse Artillery who were on parade with their guns. Without the guns, as for example at the Cenotaph service on Remembrance Sunday, the order of march is reversed.

All this might well be regarded as an anachronism in the modern world. That it is not regarded as such is evidence, I think, that people, deep down, like to feel part of a great nation with an historic past, and to be reassured that its traditions are maintained.

The rehearsal of the carriage procession is over, and now I have forty-eight hours of intensive work ahead of me. A commentary on a set-piece event like this is very different from a sporting broadcast, which is a journey into the unknown, where fluency, quick wits and knowledge of the game or sport are paramount.

The excellence of our ceremonial organisation in this country means that events usually run to time and unfold as planned; the immediate problem is to find out what *is* planned. Key documents covering the service and processions are often issued very late and commentators beg for proof copies hot off the press. It is essential, also, to find somebody – and it is surprising how difficult this is – who knows *every* detail. Most people know only their own part in the overall pattern, and it was with some relief that I 'walked the course' with the Sacrist and consulted the organist, Christopher Dearnley, about the music. Both were invaluable helpers. My notebook was getting full.

'Do you have a lot of filling in to do?' I am often asked. No, you don't; never, except once, when Prince Philip's car had a puncture in Tanzania, can I ever recall having *enough* time. It was to be no different at the Silver Jubilee; every second must count.

In television, the picture is there; the commentator annotates it. In contrast, a radio commentary has to create a picture in the mind of the listener and keep it the right way up. To do this, it is important to establish your own position clearly at the start and to relate the commentary consistently to it. Then facts and background, relevant to each phase of the event – in this case the Jubilee service – can be woven together, with the action, as it takes place. All this of course must exactly fit the time available and not obtrude on the service. Easier said than done.

My notes are my salvation, my passport to success and my lifebelt in a sea of uncertainty, if timings go awry. I stick them on cardboard for ease of handling, a separate piece for each phase of the event. These notes represent the distilled wisdom of my preparation, my final decision on what I will attempt to say and when I will say it. To anyone but myself, they must seem incomprehensible.

They consist of a series of headings, with an occasional phrase, which might be appropriate at a particular point. Those in the various processions are listed, but only key figures actually mentioned; more important is the colour, the human touches and the general impression it all makes. At the beginning and end, I usually write an incomplete sentence ... finishing it as the spirit moves me on the day. Some notes will be in red brackets, meaning they can be omitted if time is short; others, in green brackets, are for inclusion if more time is available than expected.

This method of loose but carefully arranged notes gives me the flexibility to describe faithfully what I see on the day, but also to speak concentrated and relevant sense to a tight timetable. All my work and experience goes into my notes. I will guard them carefully until finally settled into my commentary position – in this case high up in the west gallery of St Paul's.

This structure proved to be a semi-detached residence shared with my neighbour, Tom Fleming of BBC Television. While hardly an estate agent's dream, it 'afforded', as they say, an excellent, if somewhat aerial, view of St Paul's and was equipped with a table lamp and an extractor fan. However it lacked home comforts, such as plumbing. Here, my unrivalled knowledge of the Cathedral came in handy. Few knew, but I did, that half-way along the north side of the triforium was a flushing lavatory. This surprising, but priceless, information, not unlike discovering an oasis in a desert, was to make me the hero of the hour among the assorted bunch of cable layers, photographers and trumpeters whose duties made them temporary tenants of the triforium. The alternative was to follow the 500 feet of cable leading from my microphone down the spiral staircase, along the full length of the nave, and then down to the crypt, where the engineers were much more handily placed to answer the calls of nature.

My commentary box lived up to its name. My part of it was about eight feet by six feet, made of hardwood and roughly soundproofed. It had a glass front, a wide desk and two chairs. On the desk was a telephone to the engineers below, incorporating a 'cue light' system, which would be operated by my 'second pair of eyes', John Haslam,

Robert Hudson in his commentary box high up in the
west gallery of St Paul's Cathedral – it afforded an excellent,
if somewhat aerial view.

now Deputy Press Secretary to The Queen. To the right, a small television monitor set was angled so that I could see it without turning my head. Two 'lip' microphones, one for use and one in reserve, reposed on foam matting to deaden sound if they were placed on the desk too heavily. This type of microphone is held close to the mouth, cutting out all extraneous noise. John Haslam would be able to speak into my right ear without being heard on the air.

But rehearsals are under way below, so I must go down, notebook and stopwatch at the ready. Here come the Yeomen of the Guard in impeccable dark suits with black shoes; they hold their long halberds, and move with stately tread from the Great West Door, avoiding our engineers rigging their microphones across the nave. Soon the gentlemen-at-arms and the heralds will follow; mufti today, gorgeous uniforms tomorrow. At the east end, the choir suddenly bursts into song and I carefully time the hymn. It is an odd fact that if you talk over a *complete* verse of a hymn, nobody complains; but speak over *half* a verse and you will be accused of 'interrupting the singing'.

I am looking for seconds, wherever I can find them during the service, to 'signpost' ahead and identify speakers. For example, will the Archbishop of York walk to the lectern to read the lesson during, or after, the psalm? I pace it out. How much musical introduction will there be to the psalms and hymns? I check with the organist. Will the Dean wait for everyone to kneel down and the reverberating noise to subside before the opening prayer? Another ten seconds there; it is surprising how long 3000 people take to kneel.

Down in the crypt, lines are being tested and final adjustments made to some fifty microphones which will give sound to the world. What you hear on your television on these big occasions is, apart from the commentary, provided by BBC Radio.

I watch the rehearsals at ground level. What, I ask the Dean, Dr Martin Sullivan, a friendly New Zealander, will he say to The Queen when she arrives?

'I shall say,' he replies, 'it is a great honour, Your Majesty, to welcome you to St Paul's Cathedral on your Silver Jubilee' – which seemed fair enough. One couldn't argue with it.

The Queen and the Duke of Edinburgh lead the vast congregation in prayer during the Silver Jubilee Thanksgiving Service at St Paul's Cathedral, 7 June 1977.

The rehearsal is nearly over. I check the exact point at which the opening hymn will begin – when the Verger leading The Queen's procession reaches the end of the nave.

Finally a word with the State Trumpeters of the Household Cavalry. Would they please hold their trumpets to their lips for five seconds, as a warning signal, before sounding the fanfare? They will; my contacts at Trooping the Colour have their uses! They sound the fanfare again for my stopwatch; eighteen seconds.

Back to my hotel now to burn the midnight oil. Tomorrow really is the Silver Jubilee.

The room in my hotel near Liverpool Street station has a writing desk – essential, and checked in advance. Soon every inch of it is covered with orders of service, ceremonial documents, coloured pencils and ham sandwiches. Eventually my notes, wrestled into their final shape, are stuck on their bits of cardboard and I sink into bed. It is one o'clock; quite an early night. Before Lord Mountbatten's funeral, I did not go to bed at all.

Preparation, as ever, has bred confidence, so I sleep soundly until room service produces an early breakfast. Then by tube to St Paul's to find thousands lining the pavements, many wet from overnight rain. My special pass admits me, by a side door, to the engineers' hideout in the crypt. I warn them when to expect the cue light, to signal a piece of commentary, and stress that split seconds will count. Old friends; they know the form.

Then upstairs to the vastness of the nave, with the seating plan – just received – in my hand. Mr Callaghan gets a front row seat, but four former prime ministers, Messrs Macmillan, Heath, Wilson and Home, are in the sixth row. Such are the fruits of office. Mrs Thatcher is there too, but, as it were, waiting in the wings. This is 1977. I must remember to check through my binoculars that they all turn up. Someone pushes details of the royal dresses and uniforms into my hand – never available until the day itself. I add this to my bulging brief-case and prepare to tackle the winding stairs to the west gallery. On the way, I pass the television cameras, supposedly 'disguised' in sort of cardboard pillboxes. They still look like television cameras.

The Queen Mother with Prince Andrew, Prince Edward, Princess Margaret and Viscount Linley in the front pew at St Paul's Cathedral.

Up in the commentary box, I organise the desk to my liking. In the left corner stands a list of the processions, with timings. A travelling clock gives me a time check without recourse to my wrist watch. At my left elbow stands a small bottle of glycerine and lemon to ward off frogs in the throat. My precious notes are stacked in front of me. I check they are in the right order. My stopwatch is propped at an angle in its box, and the television screen flickers with rehearsal pictures. I have a sip of coffee from a flask in my brief-case, John Haslam settles in beside me, and we are ready to make contact with the outside world.

Being part of a team, as in this case, has its hazards. Control of the broadcast is in the hands of the producer in Broadcasting House. He or she may have some bright last-minute idea which will disorganise my careful preparation. As I look down on the assembling congregation, my headphones are alive with chat, instructions and a few words of 'level' for the engineers. I tell them I have never seen the tops of so many new hats in my life – a sort of milliner's dream. They seem mildly amused. At five minutes past ten, Desmond Lynam, nowadays the doyen of television sports presenters, introduces the programme. Soon the familiar voices of Alun Williams outside Buckingham Palace, Judith Chalmers, apparently stationed between the paws of a lion in Trafalgar Square, John Snagge who, remarkably, had broadcast the Silver Jubilee of George V forty-two years before, and Brian Johnston, outside St Paul's, fill my ears. I listen with interest to what is happening down the route and am jerked back to reality when Desmond cues over to me for a one-minute 'scene set'. All goes well; another sip of coffee.

Soon the first of the royal processions is leaving Buckingham Palace and, in St Paul's, those of the Speaker and the Lord Chancellor move slowly up the nave. Then come the Yeomen of the Guard, the Yeomen Warders from the Tower of London, and the Gentlemen-at-Arms to provide a brilliant frame of colour to the scene. Outside, the Guard of Honour of the Honourable Artillery Company comes marching into position – my old regiment.

The broadcast seems to be going well, augmented by the formidable experience of Godfrey Talbot and Audrey Russell in the studio; but are there, perhaps, too many recorded flashbacks of The Queen's life? I get the impression that we are as much in the past as the present.

Sitting seventy feet up in my little box as the procession approaches, I feel that fate, with a curious sense of inevitability, is about to catch up with me. Very shortly I will make or mar a broadcast which is going round the world and will for ever remain in the BBC's archives. There will be only one chance to get it right.

A solid wall of cheering brings the Gold State Coach down The Mall, through Trafalgar Square, and so on down the Strand to Temple Bar. At the rear wheel rides Prince Charles, as Colonel of the Welsh Guards, but anonymous in his black bearskin cap. In front and behind come the jingling black horses of the Sovereign's Escort. Ten bands stationed down the route play the National Anthem, softly, so as not to frighten the horses.

Now it is over to me for what should be five minutes – 'plenty of time', says a voice in my ear from the studio; I know better, thanks to my discoveries at the early morning rehearsal. Sure enough, after three minutes fifteen seconds, my monitor screen shows the Guard of Honour presenting arms and the Gold State Coach drawing up at the bottom of the steps; so it is back to Brian Johnston outside.

Now for the tricky part, as The Queen, looking, I felt, quite relieved to escape the swaying motion of the coach, comes up the steps preceded by the Lord Mayor. At this point I could do with five eyes – for my notes, the television screen, the State Trumpeters, my stopwatch and the procession waiting in the nave. John Haslam and I have only four eyes between us.

But all goes well. Antony Craxton, the Television Producer in his control van outside, keeps his cameras on The Queen at the West door, directly below and out of my sight; the Trumpeters hold their trumpets to their lips in the clearest possible signal; the fanfare takes exactly eighteen seconds, the Sacrist gives an unmistakable sign for the procession to move, and Christopher Dearnley starts the hymn at precisely the prearranged point. Into that four and a quarter minutes, hours of thought and preparation have been invested. It had been worth it. I got it right.

The Royal Family is seated in the front row, under the dome, where The Queen had sat as a little girl of nine, in a pink dress, straw hat and ankle socks, at her grandfather's Silver Jubilee in 1935. She had sung then this same processional hymn 'All people that on earth do dwell'.

Now with Prince Philip next to her in naval uniform, she sits on a scarlet and gold chair in front. A family conference had plainly taken place to avoid colour clashes. The Queen is in pink, The Queen Mother in yellow, Princess Anne in blue, the Duchess of Kent in green. Prince Charles finds kneeling with a sword too much of a problem and, very sensibly, gives it up as a bad job.

Up aloft, our cue light flickers as I use every second to signpost the way ahead and to bring the scene to life. The Archbishop of Canterbury, Dr Coggan, in a striking gold cope, ends his sermon, and two verses of the national anthem, sung with almost tangible emotion, bring the memorable service to an end.

The finish of a broadcast is as important as its start.

So what should I say of our Royal Family, now seen in one single procession as they come back down the nave towards me? 'The family firm', to quote Prince Charles. My overwhelming impression is how lucky we are to have them as part of the oldest hereditary monarchy in the world. As for The Queen herself, I suggest that we should be 'thankful for her stability and common sense, which has upheld the dignity and honour of the Crown'. That seems to match the feelings of the crowds outside, as she and Prince Philip appear at the West door. The sun comes out. Jubilation begins in earnest.

It had been an imaginative idea to arrange for The Queen to walk from St Paul's to the Guildhall for the civic luncheon. However,

RIGHT: *Brian Johnston, with his producer Roger MacDonald, walked just behind The Queen and the Lord Mayor of London, Sir Robin Gillett, during the walkabout.*

few could have envisaged its astonishing success, with security, and hooligans, taking a back seat.

Brian Johnston, behind The Queen, with a producer and an engineer with a portable transmitter, tried to get Prince Philip to say a few words on the air. 'I'd like to,' he said, 'but I can't hear myself think!'

Relaxing in the commentary box with a cup of coffee, the cheering in my headphones was deafening and my monitor screen showed the crowds packed in on either side of Cheapside, cameras at the ready, children hoisted on shoulders, Union Jacks waving, and The Queen frequently stopping for a chat – in fact, so frequently that she was late for lunch. Meanwhile, in Blackheath, exactly five people were attending an 'anti-monarchist' rally!

During her speech in reply to the Lord Mayor, Her Majesty renewed the moving pledge to the service of her people made at the age of twenty-one in, as she called them, her 'salad days'. She did not 'regret or retract' a word of it. Meanwhile, our broadcast was out and about round Britain and the world, dropping in on street parties and jollifications of all kinds. John Haslam and I, our job done, wound our way down the spiral staircase of St Paul's; a word with our devoted engineers, who seemed pleased with the way things had gone, and so out to a rather less glamorous lunch than that at the Guildhall.

Two days later, The Queen and Prince Philip visited Greenwich, where cheering drowned the church bells and the fanfares; then up river in the Port of London Authority launch, the *Nore*, with two police launches in front and six escorts in line astern. At the Tower of London, the crowds were twenty deep as the couple came ashore to much hooting of sirens. At Highbury Fields, in heavy rain, the Rolls Royce with the royal standard fluttering on the bonnet, looked more like a mobile florist's shop, as masses of flowers were piled inside. And so on, in due course, all round Britain and the Commonwealth.

What is one to make then of a Silver Jubilee – ignored by Queen Elizabeth I in 1583, but celebrated in such heart-warming style by Her Majesty Queen Elizabeth II?

Oddly perhaps, despite the pomp and ceremony, one recalls first the informality of it all. We have a genius, as a nation, for adapting

*The sun came out after the service and The Queen walked from
St Paul's to a civic luncheon at the Guildhall.*

ancient ritual to modern use, and the joy of people – on holiday and letting their hair down – seemed to blend quite naturally with the ancient pageantry. All the mystique of the monarchy – but with the common touch.

Above all, here was 'chieftainship' in action; the need to feel part of something long-lasting, secure and revered. Our Queen can trace her ancestry back some 1300 years, and the hereditary principle allows us to change our government, without fuss, under the ever-present 'umbrella' of the monarchy. For The Queen, the Silver Jubilee was a personal triumph.

For my part, I felt satisfied with what I had done, in the time available to me, and proud to have played a key part in a wonderful occasion. Everyone who could was naturally watching on television, but even at home, and certainly round the world, the radio audience was also large. Many of the letters I received made all the hard work seem worthwhile.

That year, 1977, will be remembered as the year when republicanism took a back seat. What is more, Britain's Virginia Wade won the Ladies' Singles championship at Wimbledon in the presence of The Queen. Wonders will never cease!

BUCKINGHAM PALACE AND THE BBC

RONALD ALLISON, CVO

Ronald Allison is in the unusual position of having worked not only for the BBC but also in the Press Office at Buckingham Palace. He was appointed as Press Secretary to Her Majesty The Queen in 1973 after four years as the BBC's Court Correspondent. This experience gives him the opportunity to reflect on the relationship between the BBC and the monarchy during the 1970s.

IT WAS, I SUPPOSE, inevitable that when I became Press Secretary to The Queen, after four years as the BBC's Court Correspondent, the phrase 'poacher turned gamekeeper' should leap to several editorial minds. Not that I could argue too much; indeed no journalist would deny that at times the work includes at least a little part-time poaching and while I never saw the Press Secretary's job as being to set traps for the 'poachers' there were times when I found myself flushing out photographers hiding in bushes at, say, Windsor or Balmoral.

However, I much preferred one newspaper comment at the time which, in the style of A. A. Milne, and since I was succeeding Robin Ludlow, declared:

'They're changing guard at Buckingham Palace
Robin goes out and in comes Allis ... on.'

The appointment was generally welcomed as at least a good sign that
a working journalist was moving into the Press Office. I was extremely
fortunate in being in the right place at the time The Queen and her
advisers decided to take such a step, and I had no doubts about the
style I would adopt, at least while I developed my own. Bill Heseltine
(later Sir William) had, during his years as Press Secretary, improved
Palace-press relations beyond all recognition and when he moved into
the Private Secretaries' office in 1972, it was to the regret of all
journalists who had dealt with him. His successor, Robin Ludlow,
stayed only a short time and so I inherited a Press Office still very
largely in the highly effective Heseltine mould. It included a small,
totally dedicated, extremely hard-working staff who were already
friends and who, I am glad to report, remained so after we became
colleagues.

Understandably, there was some wariness of me as a BBC man:
from one or two in the Royal Household who thought I might try to
go too far in 'opening-up' the Royal Family; from Fleet Street that I
might favour the broadcasters; and from the ITV companies, ITN in
particular, that the BBC might be given preferential treatment. I was
determined to be both as sensible as possible and totally even-handed,
and sooner than I expected I was given the opportunity to demonstrate
this.

For some months before I went to the Palace in May 1973,
rumours had persisted that the then Princess Anne was going to marry
the then Lieutenant Mark Phillips. Acting undoubtedly as he thought
best at the time, although against the advice of his colleagues in the
Press Office, Robin Ludlow had told journalists, including myself, that
there was no truth in these rumours. This had been duly reported
although most journalists, again including myself, still felt that there
was so much smoke that there must be a fire. So it proved to be.

In no time at all after taking over I was told that the Princess and
Lieutenant Phillips *were* to become engaged. No more denials came

Richard Cawston, producer and director of the major BBC *television documentary*
Royal Family *discusses a scene*
from the film with The Queen.

from the Press Office although we still had to maintain the 'no comment' stance until the time of the official announcement. This is where the skill of 'steering' comes into play, that is pointing the media in the right direction while not breaking any confidences. Quite apart from the immorality of telling lies, it is just plain stupid to deny truths that will inevitably become public knowledge but, when there are good reasons for not making an announcement until a certain time, the sensible thing is to guide speculation towards the right conclusion. It is not a good idea, however, to promote speculation. As it turned out, by the time of the official announcement of the engagement, everyone was expecting it, but the Palace Press Office had held its line and everyone seemed happy.

So it was that, throughout the summer of 1973, my colleagues and I were totally occupied with arranging the coverage of a royal wedding that seemed to have caught most people's imagination. Thankfully, organising the event itself was nothing to do with the Press Office. That considerable responsibility fell on the Lord Chamberlain's Office, together with the Dean and Chapter of Westminster Abbey, the Metropolitan Police, the Department of the Environment, the Armed Services and many others – to say nothing of the two families involved.

The team at the top of the Lord Chamberlain's Office at the time was the Lord Chamberlain himself, the late Lord Maclean, the Comptroller, Sir Eric Penn, and his colleague, Sir John Johnston. As ever, the result of their thoroughness, flair and total attention to detail was a day of flawless pageantry, shared by tens of thousands in London and by millions watching and listening around the world.

My close involvement in it made me all the sadder when some sixteen years later, the Princess and her husband decided to separate but, at the time, the wedding and all that preceded it was hugely enjoyable. Darned hard work dealing with the media of the world but, above all, fun.

On such occasions it is not only simpler but necessary to go in for 'pooling', the system whereby only a limited number of journalists, photographers, camera crews and technicians is allowed into specific areas. The chosen few then share their words and pictures with their colleagues. Traditionally the BBC had covered all the great national and state occasions, first for radio and then, since the Coronation in 1953, for television as well; but by 1973 ITV and IRN were well established and well respected as public service broadcasters, albeit commercially funded. Together then, we planned for these organisations to provide the world's broadcasters with the sound and the pictures basic to their own coverage. In fact, the BBC took total responsibility for the sound feeds for both radio and television from Westminster Abbey, and the BBC also looked after the many overseas commentators who worked 'off-tube', that is by watching the coverage on television monitors at BBC Television Centre and adding their commentaries at that point.

More than anything the planning involved answering a variety of requests. 'Can we put a camera behind the altar?' 'No.' 'May we track up a side aisle as the processions move along the main aisle?' 'Yes.' 'Where do we need to be to see the choir?' 'There,' – wherever 'there' might be. And so on. Parking the outside broadcast vehicles, running the cables, issuing the identification passes, building the soundproof commentary boxes; every matter of detail, seemingly small or obviously big, is a matter of supreme importance to those immediately concerned. And has to be treated as such.

So, too, with the newspaper journalists and the stills photographers, but their needs are certainly more easily met than those of the broadcasters. At least, the physical needs. The quest for information is another matter!

But back to the broadcasters. The American networks, as they did later for the two royal weddings of the 1980s, turned up in force. Unable to have their own cameras in the Abbey they built studios outside the Palace and were provided with as many camera positions as possible along the route of the processions. NBC, with Barbara Walters as their 'front-person', had, as I recall, the largest contingent but CBS and ABC were not far behind. Most other broadcasting organisations were less ambitious and relied almost entirely on the coverage provided by the BBC.

All the foreign correspondents and reporters were briefed by myself and by officials from Westminster Abbey and the Lord Chamberlain's Office but they also had excellent teach-ins from Antony Craxton, who was masterminding the BBC's television coverage and from Tom Fleming, who was the commentator.

When it came to briefing overseas correspondents, there really was no substitute for going straight to basics and spelling out the information in large block letters. I say this not disparagingly but realistically; many of the journalists, only in Britain for the wedding, simply did not have the background information that normally can be taken for granted – and why should they? So: the relationships within the family? (No, Princess Margaret is not the Queen's aunt, she is her sister); the route from Buckingham Palace to Westminster Abbey? (No, it will not go past the American Embassy in Grosvenor Square); the form of an Anglican wedding service? (Yes, the bride will be escorted up the aisle by her father) and so on. Every detail imaginable – and some not. (No, I don't know what the Princess will be wearing at bedtime on her wedding day!)

It was all worthwhile, because the Palace Press Office, wanted the commentators and writers to get it right. So briefs were prepared and questions answered, endlessly – details of the buildings, the route, the service, the carriages, the Lord Chamberlain's Office, the flowers, the cake, the families, the menus and, though not before the event, the dress. Oh the dress! For every question about protocol or timings, about Mark Phillips and the bridesmaids, there were a dozen about the dress. And all that could be said was – 'wait and see'.

The dress – and the honeymoon. I knew where the honeymoon would be spent; I was under orders not to say, at least not until the first destination had been reached. It was the familiar game of cat and mouse, but eventually the couple reached Princess Alexandra's home in Richmond Park, where they spent the first night of the honeymoon comparatively free of close press attention. Nevertheless such attention was not too far behind.

Antony Craxton along with Bob Service of Thames Television who was producing ITV's coverage, at times seemed to have become my almost inseparable companions and indeed Antony in particular, with his vast experience, was an enormous help to me. Overall though the Royal Wedding of 1973 demonstrated not only how well the close links with the BBC could work to the latter's advantage but how they could do so to the benefit of many others as well.

If, to get me started in the Press Office as it were, the wedding of Princess Anne was the biggest single event of my time there, the most ambitious, enjoyable and rewarding period was 1977 – Silver Jubilee year.

In the early planning stages not everyone, including some members of the Government, was persuaded that the country was ready for a major programme of celebrations. Indeed The Queen herself, mindful of the economic situation at the time, was extremely anxious to avoid ostentation or unnecessary expenditure, and in this her usual common sense and uncanny instinct was quite right. Equally correct, however, were those advisers who sensed the mood of the country – the mood of the Commonwealth, in fact – and who prepared, without ostentation and undue extravagance, a programme that took The Queen and the Duke of Edinburgh to all parts of the United Kingdom (including Northern Ireland) and to the Commonwealth countries in Australasia and the South Pacific, the Caribbean and Canada.

For much of the time it was a celebration by the people, who turned out in their millions to greet The Queen on her drives and walk-abouts, who organised thousands of street parties and who associated themselves, through television and radio, with the more formal events.

By an Andover of the Queen's Flight, by the royal train, by car, in *Britannia*, even, in Northern Ireland, by helicopter, the royal couple travelled throughout the United Kingdom in a unique royal progress. When King George V celebrated his Silver Jubilee in 1935 the people demonstrated their feelings and affection by coming to London. Over forty years later The Queen went to her people, almost wherever they were. It was a triumphant, moving year.

For the Press Office staff, all six of us, with a little extra help, it was a year of almost non-stop activity and travel. I was away from home

A lighthearted moment during the filming of Royal Family.

for over half the year. Finally on 2 November 1977, I accompanied The Queen as she flew home from Barbados in Concorde – her first flight in that aircraft – after having begun the year marshalling the photographers at a service in Windsor Chapel to commemorate the accession itself before the royal party left for the South Pacific. (There, incidentally, in Papua New Guinea I met my first cannibal. At least that's how this cheerful, very old man was introduced!)

I have no idea how many reporters, photographers and camera crews were accredited during the year, nor how many programmes of events were issued, briefings given and how many telephone calls were answered! It was a hectic time and there were certainly occasions when I wished Australian or New Zealand reporters took some note of the time difference between their countries and Britain! Every time The Queen was out on a visit, though, it all became totally worthwhile, with everyone, journalists and police included, joining in the fun. It was a year of flowers, as bouquet after bouquet of freshly picked daffodils or roses were thrust upon The Queen – flowers and the occasional Mars bar! After each royal visit that year the wards of the local hospitals were festooned with the flowers that had been passed on to them!

Radio and television did Silver Jubilee year proud. Some wonderful images, some splendid commentating and reporting, excellent scripting – all accurately and faithfully matched the occasions.

Throughout my five years in the Press Office, the BBC was the one single organisation we dealt with most often. This was not favouritism, merely in the course of events. After all, the BBC produces The Queen's annual broadcast to the Commonwealth, it covers all the major royal occasions on both radio and television. It maintains a Royal Liaison Office, through which are routed, in theory anyway, all requests for access to royal occasions. It appoints, although not on a totally full-time basis, a Court Correspondent (in my time I combined the job with that of Television News Sports Correspondent) and there is almost always a documentary programme or an interview with a member of the Royal Family in the making or at the planning stage. All this, together with the almost daily arrangements made for national

ABOVE: *Sir Huw Wheldon in Westminster Hall at the Palace of Westminster filming* Royal Heritage. *There were major contributions from The Queen, the Duke of Edinburgh and The Queen Mother.*

RIGHT: *A television cameraman always has to dress for the occasion — top hat and tails for the State Opening of Parliament!*

and regional programmes to cover events and visits – liaising with the Central Office of Information, issuing the passes, briefing the reporters, generally trying to smooth the way – keep the Palace, Broadcasting House and the Television Centre very much in touch.

The relationship, of course, depends very much on personalities, and here I was extremely fortunate in those with whom I had to deal. Moving as I had done from the BBC, men such as Peter Dimmock, Cliff Morgan, Antony Craxton, Richard Cawston, Robert Hudson, John Haslam and Bob Burrows and some of their indispensable assistants – Jane Astell and Barbara Saxton, for instance – had all been colleagues and friends and this was a tremendous advantage. I must say, though, that it needed just a little adjustment on the part of one or two when they found themselves having to deal with someone from *News*! Not that it ever showed too much and I always relished the occasional touches of 'Beeb arrogance'!

Following the success in 1969 of the documentary film, *Royal Family*, its producer Richard Cawston, who was Head of BBC Television Documentaries, had taken over responsibility for The Queen's Christmas broadcast, transmitted, as you might expect, on Christmas Day, but for reasons of logistics and distribution, recorded earlier each December. Special filming exclusively for use in the broadcast often takes place throughout the year but invariably the text is subject to last minute alterations. The recording itself usually takes place in a temporary studio set up in a ground floor room in the Palace, although on one occasion The Queen spoke from beside the lake in the Palace gardens, using a small stone to illustrate the 'ripple effect' of deeds, good and bad.

In Jubilee year, 1977, Richard Cawston acted as Executive Producer on *Royal Heritage*, a series about the treasures in the Royal Collection and the buildings that house them. The series was produced by Michael Gill, of *Civilisation* and *America* renown, presented by the late Sir Huw Wheldon as only he could have done, and all based on essays written by the historian Sir Jack Plumb. It was a most successful venture, the result of co-operation again between the Palace (particularly the Lord Chamberlain's Office) and the BBC, with major

Prince Edward made a surprise visit to the BBC on
April Fool's Day where he took part in
Radio 1's breakfast programme presented by Mike Smith.

contributions from The Queen, Prince Philip and Queen Elizabeth The
Queen Mother. The programmes were extremely popular at home and
were also widely distributed around the world. In America a ninety-
minute compilation was shown on NBC and the entire series on PBS.

The Queen also appeared in another documentary film which

gave me much personal pleasure. *Royal Garden* was produced for his own company by Bill Travers, and shot as it was season by season throughout an entire year, it beautifully revealed that in the heart of London the gardens of Buckingham Palace were in effect an important nature reserve. After seeing a rough cut of the film I telephoned Bryan Cowgill, then Controller of BBC 1, to tell him of a 'must'. Bryan viewed, bought and transmitted the film; the *Radio Times* having the chance once again of a royal cover, the *Radio Times* took it!

So much has changed at the Press Office and in the media since the early post-war royal tours were covered for the wireless with such elegance by Wynford Vaughan-Thomas, Godfrey Talbot and Audrey Russell, backed up by the expertise of the engineering and outside broadcasts staff. In all the turmoil of the last half-century, however, at least two British institutions have survived. One, the monarchy, seems secure enough as it sensibly moves along, if not absolutely up with the times, only a very short way behind. The other, the BBC, cannot be so certain of its future. If anything *is* done, however, to endanger the standards it has set and, by and large, maintained, it will be to the nation's loss.

It is not part of the BBC's function to sustain any one system of government, but in the way in which it has covered the Royal Family and its activities, personal and constitutional, over the years it has certainly contributed much to the awareness and appreciation of our constitutional monarchy by people in the United Kingdom, the Commonwealth and elsewhere and that, in my opinion, has been well worth doing.

Equally, it is not part of the Palace Press Office's function to favour any one broadcasting organisation and I am sure that the satellite companies, maybe Channel Five too, will find out, as have the ITV companies, that it does not. It will continue to be the case, though, I am sure, that Palace-BBC relations will be close and rewarding, as the one seeks to honestly and entertainingly record the doings of the other and all possible help is given to achieve that aim.

THE ROYAL WEDDING – 29 JULY 1981

TOM FLEMING, OBE

The marriage of His Royal Highness The Prince of Wales to Lady Diana Spencer in St Paul's Cathedral on 29 July 1981 was evidence, if it were needed, of the esteem in which the British Royal Family is held throughout the world. The day was one of goodwill shared by all those who watched in their homes and those who crowded on to the streets of London. It was witnessed through the medium of television by an estimated 750 million people and the television commentator in St Paul's Cathedral was Tom Fleming. He remembers this unique occasion vividly.

HISTORY, SOMEONE ONCE SAID, is what is going on under your nose while you are making plans about something else! History can also be what you see happening before your very eyes, when the circumstances and the participants dictate that a particular event is likely to be remembered in years to come as having some significance in a nation's life.

The commentator on royal events is aware of being a privileged person. He is entrusted with a mass of confidential information about the timing and mechanics of a royal occasion, from which he extracts the essential details relevant to his trade, and he has access to parts of public (and private) buildings which the ordinary citizen never sees. In fact, a commentator over the years acquires an intimate knowledge of castle turrets, dark passageways and dusty lumber-strewn cathedral galleries which he shares only with stonemasons, roofing contractors, and in the grim later decades of the twentieth century, indefatigable police 'sniffer' dogs. He should have an aptitude for endless dizzy-making turnpike stairs, and an addiction to climbing high vertical ladders with a brief-case in one hand and an official pass clenched between the teeth! He (or she – the late Audrey Russell had her share of clambering over church furnishings during royal weddings!) is also aware of rubbing shoulders with another kind of history – the history that relates to the fascinating evolution of broadcasting itself.

I remember very vividly, as a small boy of seven, listening in my father's study in Edinburgh to the first royal wedding to be broadcast. It was November 1934, and the occasion was the marriage of King George V's youngest son, the Duke of Kent, to Princess Marina of Greece in Westminster Abbey. (A request by the British Broadcasting Company – as it then was – to broadcast the wedding of the Duke and Duchess of York – later King George VI and Queen Elizabeth – had been turned down.) I listened in 1934 to a 'wireless' set operated by dry and wet batteries with a cone-shaped loudspeaker which hung above my father's bookcase. (We had no electricity in the house.) I had never been to a wedding, and I had never crossed the Scottish border, far less visited London. There was a sense of history from the first words of the opening announcement. The silk-smooth voice of the BBC's Chief Announcer Stuart Hibberd told us in tones of high drama that the broadcast would be heard 'throughout these islands' and on the Empire Service world-wide. There was a breathless hand-over to the commentator outside the Abbey, Howard Marshall (how many of you recall his voice of dark brown velvet?), who began with the momentous phrase: 'Well . . . there's nothing very much happening here . . .' From that point things could only get better. I was enchanted by the vivid scenes described by excited voices and colourful words;

the horse-drawn processions, the cheering crowds, the solemnity of the service within the Abbey, the peals of bells, the sounds of rejoicing as the Glass Coach set off back to Buckingham Palace. For me it was like listening to a two-hour long story. For the BBC it was a splendid rehearsal for the celebration of King George V's Silver Jubilee six months later, in May 1935.

One of my own small claims to having a peripheral share in broadcasting history dates from almost thirty-nine years after that first wedding broadcast. The wedding of Princess Anne (now The Princess Royal) took place in Westminster Abbey on 14 November 1973. It was the first occasion on which a royal wedding was televised in colour. Now, at last, people at home could see such an event in more detail than those who were present by invitation. The commentator's job had become one of adding essential footnotes (and mentioning colours now and then for those who still had black-and-white sets), filling in the background to the sequence of happenings, and capturing the essential mood of the occasion without imposing a lot of personal opinions. It was also the first occasion when the description of the *bridegroom's* dress was handed to a commentator in a sealed envelope and marked 'Embargoed by the Ministry of Defence until seen on screen'! The reason was that Captain Mark Phillips was wearing for the first time a specially designed full dress uniform of his regiment. A comparatively new regiment, The Queen's Dragoon Guards was formed from the amalgamation of two old cavalry regiments and a new full dress uniform had not until then been deemed necessary. When I opened the envelope in my eyrie in the triforium of Westminster Abbey, I found that Captain Phillips was wearing 'a cavalry tunic, cross-belt, *overalls* and *Wellington boots*'. Although this was a perfectly accurate description of cavalry trousers and footgear, I thought it might sound a little odd to viewers if reported verbatim!

His Royal Highness The Prince of Wales celebrated his twenty-fifth birthday on the day of his sister's wedding. Almost eight years later, in the high summer of 1981, his own marriage with Lady Diana Spencer was to take place in the original and spectacular setting of St Paul's Cathedral. By his choice of the Cathedral Church of the

Commonwealth, on the summit of Ludgate Hill, Prince Charles was 'being his own man' and creating a precedent in terms of royal weddings. He was to be the first Prince of Wales to be married (while holding that style and title) for over a century. Prince Albert ('Bertie', later King Edward VII) married the beautiful Danish Princess Alexandra in St George's Chapel, Windsor on 10 March 1863. His mother, Queen Victoria, widowed two years previously and still in deep mourning, watched discreetly from the window of Edward IV's Chantry Chapel which looks down on the high altar of the main chapel. (I have many times commentated on royal occasions happy and sad from the selfsame window.) Queen Victoria had been married in the Chapel Royal, St James's Palace, in 1849, as was her grandson Prince George, Duke of York (afterwards King George V), over half a century later. Only in our own century have royal weddings ceased to be small family occasions. The customary venue became Westminster Abbey – a royal 'peculiar', that is, a collegiate church with strong links to the Crown. With the advent of broadcasting, such ceremonies came to be shared by millions throughout the world. By the time of Princess Anne's wedding the television audience, world-wide, was estimated at 500 million. Now, for the marriage of the Prince of Wales in July 1981, an unimaginable 'congregation' of 750 million viewers was likely.

I can well imagine that all The Queen's children have longed to be married in a quiet country church, surrounded by family and close personal friends, without the inquisitive stare of press and television cameras, and far from the glare of television lights. All have so far graciously accepted that such a human and understandable preference is 'not on'. Prince Charles and his bride-to-be were both quiet, shy and private people. But the Prince decided with characteristic flair and imagination that if his marriage to the girl of his choice was to be shared by a sixth of the world's population, it was going to be an occasion the world would long remember. If, because he was Heir to the Throne, there had to be a huge guest list of international, Commonwealth, and European representatives, there was also going to be plenty of space for their individual circles of good friends, and for loyal members of staff from the Royal Households and estates. If there was going to be music, it had to be a musical celebration of outstanding proportions and style. It was.

Westminster Abbey is quite small and dark, although its recent renovations have made it spectacularly beautiful. For the impressive Coronation ceremony it is virtually turned into a theatre (and the area where the enthronement takes place is called just that) by building surrounding stands within the Abbey and an annexe beyond the West Door. Prince Charles chose St Paul's, which is massive, light and spacious. It was associated in his mind with recent happy national and Commonwealth occasions: the celebration of Her Majesty The Queen's Silver Jubilee in 1977, and the celebration of Her Majesty Queen Elizabeth The Queen Mother's eightieth birthday in 1980. It could seat almost 3000, and the cohorts of music-makers which the Prince envisaged – musicians from three orchestras and the Bach Choir – could be tucked into the north transept and still leave room for several hundred guests there as well. The Queen, attached by sentiment to the Abbey where her own wedding took place and, of course, her Coronation, too, was nonetheless pleased to give her consent.

The 'betrothal' of the Prince of Wales to Lady Diana Spencer, the nineteen-year-old daughter of the Earl Spencer and the Honourable Mrs Shand Kydd, was announced by Buckingham Palace on 24 February 1981. The Lord Chamberlain, Lord Maclean, made the announcement during an investiture. At the same time, during a debate on marriage in the General Synod, the Archbishop of Canterbury intervened to make a similar announcement. On 25 February, Lady Diana moved from her shared flat in the Old Brompton Road to Clarence House, the London home of The Queen Mother, and gave up her job at the Young England kindergarten in Pimlico. On 3 March it was announced that the couple had chosen St Paul's Cathedral for their marriage on 29 July. On 4 March BBC Television announced its seven-hour coverage of 'The Wedding of the Century'.

There were less than five months of hectic planning ahead. On the day, seventy-six overseas broadcasting organisations would be clamouring for BBC pictures and sound, sixty-five cameras would be deployed, sixteen outside broadcast units (including units from Wales, Northern Ireland and Scotland) would be linked to Television Centre, and some 200 staff would be positioned from the inner quadrangle of Buckingham Palace to the high altar of St Paul's, and all the way to Waterloo Station for the honeymoon departure in the late afternoon. All this in a month when the BBC was committed to finding units and skilled personnel to cover the fourth test match, international athletics and glorious Goodwood, and the royal fireworks from Hyde Park, Caernarfon, Balmoral and Althorp (the Spencer family home) on the eve of the wedding itself.

My admiration has always been unbounded for the BBC's engineering managers who plan the technical complexities of covering a major 'event'. The skill and experience of an outstanding generation of engineers brought the Corporation to its well-deserved pre-eminence in the field of 'outside' broadcasting, as it is called in a rather old-fashioned way. They not only have to plan with great ingenuity, they have to deliver the goods on the day and, in addition, on an occasion such as a royal wedding, back every sound and vision circuit with a stand-by facility. The sixth-floor people refer to a 'Grade One' broadcast. The rest of us talk about 'belt and braces', the double insurance against the unspeakable!

The commentator's job in the weeks before a great event is rather less obviously rewarding. He gets involved (sometimes, as in this case, with the aid of a first-class researcher) in amassing a wealth of relevant facts. Here the good commentator uses his creative imagination and collects also an immense amount of *irrelevant* information and background which will come in handy if things don't go according to plan! The next bit of the operation is painstaking and solitary: absorbing the facts somewhere between the ears. It is a lot like cramming for 'O' levels, and every bit as glamorous. The architectural embellishments

RIGHT: *The Prince of Wales and Lady Diana Spencer were interviewed by Angela Rippon (BBC) and Andrew Gardner (ITN) before their wedding. It was shown on both channels at 6 p.m., 28 July 1981.*

of the buildings along the processional route, the curriculum vitae of the Archbishop of Canterbury, the units of the armed forces finding the Guards of Honour, the kind of trees that grow along The Mall (and when they were planted) are facts that are not likely to change before the great day. Seating plans and ecclesiastical processions are quite likely to change in the last twenty-four hours. Elderly clerics fall ill, or guests from abroad are prevented from attending by travel problems or some political upheaval in a far country. However well you do your 'homework', essential facts pour into your hand on the eve of any great event, and have to be poured into your head in the few hours of darkness when saner human beings are sleeping. On the day itself open-carriage processions may have to be altered because of adverse weather conditions, and horses may have to be switched at the last moment because of indisposition or undue friskiness. A hot line to the Royal Mews is a must. Viewers get very irate if you can't tell them the name of the grey gelding to the right of the postilion!

Among my happiest memories of royal occasions across forty years are the early morning rehearsals of carriage processions. Often, on weekdays in winter, they take place before dawn. While London sleeps on, a solemn ritual proceeds. The Queen's Guard turns out and comes to attention, a band plays the National Anthem, and figures in greatcoats salute in a suitably dignified manner while an empty coach, its blinds drawn, moves across the forecourt of Buckingham Palace. It is all part of the meticulously professional preparation which makes national events in this country the envy of the world. But it is also quite amusing and endearing.

The rehearsal of the military ceremonial and the complicated sequence of carriage processions for the Royal Wedding in 1981 took place on the Sunday morning preceding the wedding day. At 7 a.m. a Guard of Honour, a hundred strong, formed by The Queen's Guard and provided by the Prince of Wales's Company, First Battalion, Welsh Guards (the regiment of footguards of which the Prince is Colonel), marched with their Regimental Band and the Battalion's Corps of Drums from Colour Court, St James's Palace, to the forecourt of Buckingham Palace. Five minutes after the Guard of Honour had

Lady Diana Spencer arrives at St Paul's Cathedral and the moment the world has been waiting for – the first look at the dress designed by David and Elizabeth Emanuel.

formed up, two Escorts of Household Cavalry arrived at the Palace from Knightsbridge. No sooner were they in position than all the carriages from the Royal Mews, just around the corner, were driven across the forecourt and through the southern archway into the inner quadrangle. With my producer Michael Lumley and his assistant, Jennie Birkett, I then sped by car to St Paul's where fifteen minutes later the first arrivals were to be rehearsed. A car from St James's Palace (on the day there would be five cars carrying 'minor Royals' – close relatives of the Royal Family), and a car from Ave Maria Lane (on the day, three cars would carry the Lord Mayor and his retinue, representing the City of London, on the two-minute journey) arrived one after the other at the steps of the Cathedral. It was still only 8 a.m.

At 8.05, the six landaus of The Queen's carriage procession, accompanied by four divisions of the Household Cavalry Escort, turned sharply from St Paul's Churchyard at the top of Ludgate Hill to halt behind the statue of Queen Anne. (She stands with her back to Wren's masterpiece looking towards Ludgate Circus and Fleet Street beyond.) The indefatigable Sir John Miller, a trusted and much loved royal servant, had been Crown Equerry for twenty years by 1981. He jumped down from the Semi-state Landau, consulted with Mews officials and staff, glanced at a stopwatch, got into a car, and sped back to Buckingham Palace. Forty minutes later he arrived with the bridegroom's carriage. The same procedure: off down Ludgate Hill, to return forty minutes later with the bride's Glass Coach. His responsibility was to oversee the carriage processions. He was a great respecter of horses, and had unquenchable enthusiasm for his job. He wanted to see at first hand any problems his coachmen or postillion riders (or, come to that, his horses) might encounter en route. His third and last arrival was at 9.25 a.m. By 10.05 the bride and bridegroom's procession had been formed, and The Queen's procession reformed at St Paul's, and both set off within five minutes of each other for the Palace. The return journey took twenty minutes. By 11 a.m. Sir John was off again, leaving the Palace with a Travelling Escort of Household Cavalry for Waterloo Station on the final leg of the carriage rehearsal. We had travelled by car to Westminster Bridge. We alighted and walked the rest of the honeymoon departure route (through streets one isn't often called to comment on) and up the vehicle ramp to the station itself. Already, as we drove from St Paul's, Ludgate Hill was filled with people in carnival spirit. Some had come to preview the horses and the carriages. But others had set up camp, and intended to be in residence near their vantage points for the next three days!

By twelve noon, Sir John's horses had gone to their Sunday nosebags, and Mike Lumley, Jennie Birkett, our intrepid researcher Helen Holmes (her brief-case by now a weight-lifter's nightmare!) and I repaired to Broadcasting House for a quick canteen lunch.

At 1.30 p.m. we were due to brief the commentators and representatives of overseas broadcasting organisations in the Concert Hall. (Thirty-three years before I had had the easier task of introducing the Palm Court Orchestra from the same stage, as a Light Programme announcer!) It is always fun to explain the quaint terms of our British ceremonial to colleagues from other countries, and to share a few tricks of instant recognition one has accumulated over the years (plumes on hats, the numbers of buttons on tunics). On this occasion the Americans seemed obsessed with how our cameras would deal with an assassination attempt, or how we would cover riots in The Mall. It was a sad reminder of the kind of stories television screens across the world too often have to depict. A lighter moment came from trying to explain to a correspondent from the Far East that a 'minor Royal' had nothing to do with being on the executive of the National Union of Mineworkers.

That evening there was a first rehearsal of the orchestra formed by musicians from the Royal Opera House, Covent Garden, the English Chamber Orchestra and the Philharmonia Orchestra. The Bach Choir, too, was in attendance at St Paul's. Sir David Willcocks, Director of the Royal School of Music (and of the Bach Choir), was in overall charge of the music for the wedding and had chosen the last aria and chorus from Handel's *Samson* to be performed during the signing of the registers. (Handel used to love to play the organ at St Paul's late into the evening in his shirt sleeves.) The aria was 'Let the bright seraphim in burning row their loud uplifted angel trumpets blow'. The soloist was Kiri Te Kanawa (who was practising singing with a hat on). She was accompanied by John Wallace (trumpet) and John Scott (organ continuo). The chorus was 'Let their celestial concerts all unite'. Choir and orchestra did just that, and filled the mighty dome with a rich paeon of sound. Surely Wednesday 29 July would be as unforgettable as the Prince was hoping. Sir Colin Davis conducted

Elgar's 'Pomp and Circumstance March No. 4', and there was a shiver up the spine. Christopher Dearnley, Organist and Director of Music at St Paul's, played Jeremiah Clark's 'Trumpet Voluntary' with the orchestra conducted by Sir David Willcocks. Together they had made this arrangement, which was to accompany the bridal procession. The hairs rose on the nape of one's neck. And that was in an empty cathedral, late in the evening, without the bride!

On Monday afternoon there were further treats in store. At 2.30 p.m. the Choir of St Paul's and the Gentlemen and Children of Her Majesty's Chapels Royal stood together in the choir stalls with their luxuriant carvings by Wren's immigrant Dutch master-craftsman Grinling Gibbons. (He had his workshop just down Ludgate Hill three centuries ago.) They were to sing for the first time a wedding anthem commissioned from Professor William Mathias especially for the occasion. It was a setting of words from Psalm 67: 'Let the people praise Thee, O God'. Christopher Dearnley was at the organ, Barry Rose, Master of the Choir at St Paul's, conducted, and the composer listened, seated in the crossing. Also in the Cathedral (as he was at every rehearsal) was the bride's father the Earl Spencer, and Sir John Betjeman, the Poet Laureate, sadly by then in a wheelchair. In his younger days he had helped save St Paul's as a member of the firefighting team during the incendiary raids of the Second World War. Everyone found the soaring young voices of the choristers touchingly beautiful. Then they were joined by the trumpeters of the Royal Military School of Music, Kneller Hall, for Parry's great anthem 'I was glad'. Christopher Dearnley's new setting of Versicles and Responses for the Lesser Litany was sung by the Sacrist, the Reverend Michael Moxon, and the choir. Finally, the two hymns: 'Christ is made the sure Foundation' to the tune which Henry Purcell called after the place where he once was organist, and where his remains now lie,

RIGHT: *A quick smile from Prince Charles as his bride joins him having walked up the aisle with her father, the Earl Spencer. Prince Andrew looks on.*

Westminster Abbey (a nice touch, I thought) and 'I vow to thee my country' in the setting by Gustav Holst, a favourite hymn of the bride's from schooldays, were rehearsed. The choristers and lay-clerks, the Children and Gentlemen, were dismissed, and at 4 p.m. the State Trumpeters played through the fanfare that would greet the bride at the Great West Door, and then climbed aloft to sound the new fanfare 'The Rejoicing' by Major Richards of the Life Guards, from the Whispering Gallery high in the dome. What an unbelievable sound! This was to greet the procession of the bride and bridegroom as they came arm in arm through the choir at the end of the service. The actual marriage ceremony was to take place on a raised carpeted platform to the west of the choir and under the dome within the crossing. But now at 4.30, the Cathedral was cleared. The principal players were coming to rehearse their parts. They would have half an hour of something approaching privacy with just forty-two hours until count-down.

For the BBC production staff, engineers and camera crews there were some twenty-six waking hours remaining for all the hectic refinements of lighting, checking the communications between cameramen in their often isolated locations on top of buildings, or behind screens in the Cathedral itself, and the producer in his mobile control van parked in the precincts; between Mike Lumley at St Paul's and his colleagues in their control vans (or scanners) at Buckingham Palace, The Mall, the Strand and Temple Bar; between St Paul's and Television Centre where the forty-five international commentators were ensconced.

It was after the main facilities check on the eve of the wedding, and during our vital camera rehearsal (when for the first time a commentator actually sees through the eyes of the cameras the processional route he has trudged so often on foot), that I was aware of footsteps climbing the rungs of the tall ladder that led to the com-

RIGHT: *The Queen and the Earl Spencer on their way back to Buckingham Palace after the service. Hundreds of thousands of people lined the streets to cheer the processions.*

mentary box perched high above the west gallery of St Paul's. There was so much going on that I didn't even look round. Alex Thomas, one of our senior stage managers and a friend over many years, was positioned at the door of the commentary box to 'keep the ground', as our army colleagues might say. He raised one of my padded head-phones and whispered, 'Alistair Cooke'. By the time I had extricated myself from microphone cables and bits of paper the distinguished broadcaster was commencing his descent, and from the bottom of the ladder looked up, smiled, and in his most relaxed *Letter from America* delivery said, 'I can see you're busy!' I'd love to have had a talk with him. I wondered what he thought of the American network who had flown over a jet-load of American television personalities and placed them, facing camera, in a sort of perspex studio built on to the front of an office building overlooking St Paul's. You could see the steps leading up to the Great West Door in the background just over their shoulders. There they sat chatting amongst themselves 'in vision' about the wedding that was going to take place behind their backs! I have always passionately subscribed to the old BBC tradition that the commentator must never come between the viewer and the event which is being covered. The illusion one wishes to create in and for the viewer is that he or she is actually *there* in person. Therefore the better the commentary, the less anyone is aware of it.

By the evening before the wedding, St Paul's looked absolutely breath-taking. Commander Charles Shears, the Registrar and Receiver (or lay administrator) of the Cathedral, who had been singularly patient and helpful to us, allowed himself the faintest hint of a smile. The retired naval officer was proud of his ship. The summer flowers in their profusion filled the air with heady perfume. Lilies, roses, carnations, gladioli, chrysanthemums, hydrangeas in a delicate translation from white through cream to soft gold. Some of the arrangements were eighteen feet tall. On the huge columns which support the dome were hung Prince of Wales's feathers made of pampas grass with fresh, dried and silk flowers. These emblems were ten feet high and six feet across.

Between the pillars of the nave, garlands were suspended like giant daisy-chains linking the west door to the centre crossing under the dome. The Ladies Flower Committee of St Paul's shared with the Worshipful Company of Gardeners and Longmans, the city florists, the triumph of such a simple and beautiful display on such an enormous scale. Some of the flowers came from Windsor Castle. The television lighting by Bryan Wilkes, it has to be said, further enhanced the splendour of the setting which now awaited the pageantry of the coming day.

5.15 a.m. 'This is your alarm call' was the unromantic dawn chorus that awoke me in my hotel room on the Strand. 'Always sling your hammock within walking distance of the commentary point' is the maxim which hangs on a rusty nail in my brain. If all known methods of private and public transport let you down, the theory is you can still get there in time on the hoof! Quick bath. On with the striped trousers and the swallow-tail coat. (It's not that you dress for passing pigeons looking through the windows of the west gallery, but you may have to mingle with guests while checking last minute changes to the seating plan in the nave.) Clean handkerchief? Money? Police pass and identification? Stopwatch? Pen … pencil … throat pastilles … camera script and commentary notes in brief-case? Police pass? Oh! spectacles … two pairs just in case … well, one in a case, the other in a top pocket. Notes? Identification? Coat? (No. The forecast's good, and it's not my morning dress!) Police pass? A second ring on the bedside telephone calls a halt to the hysterical check-list. 'Your car is at the door.' Five minutes early − 6.15. O me of little faith! Police pass?

The BBC had sent no mere car, but a shining limousine with chauffeur in a grey peaked cap. (At this stage of the day I'm a valuable commodity.) Sparse crowds to witness this departure. We have a brush with a passing road-sweeper! The driver takes ingenious back-street short-cuts. They are actually long-cuts but he promises to get us there on schedule by 6.30. Brief-case? Spectacles? Police pass? (I should put it somewhere sensible, but then it would be lost for ever!) St Paul's − and still five minutes early. He's going to park the limousine underground facing the exit for a quick get-away at 2 p.m. It's not that he anticipates the commentary is going to be *that bad*; it's to get me quickly to the Victoria Memorial for the honeymoon departure.

My first question of the day is 'Where is the riggers' van?' They always have coffee on the go. This is really the last chance to wish the cameramen, the sound and vision engineers, the colleagues in the mobile recording vans, and the production staff good luck in person. Outside broadcasts are very much a team effort. Nobody's contribution is less important than anyone else's. It's live and it's dangerous, and we're all in it together, trying to create something memorable and worthwhile. From 7.15 a.m. all the cameras and sound links are in rehearsal. By 7.45 a.m. they are making live contributions to the build-up programme coming from Television Centre. Barbara Griggs joins me in the commentary box to describe the fashion scene. (What a relief! I always remember the male commentator who described Princess Margaret as wearing an 'off the face' hat!) Helen Holmes is making a quick call to the Royal Mews enquiring after the health of the horses. At 9.45 a.m. we go on the air with four hours of live transmission joined by viewers in sixty countries.

As with all great occasions, you plan, prepare, eat and sleep them for months beforehand. When the moment arrives, four hours slip by in a flash. Michael Lumley, the overall producer, and I had talked long and in detail about the approach. Basically it came to this: we were telling a story. Here was Buckingham Palace: the home of the bridegroom and his family. Here was St Paul's, on a hilltop three miles away. Here was Clarence House, where the bride was getting ready. She would be joined by her father, and by the bridesmaids and pages. The groom's family would foregather at the Palace. In St Paul's the family of nations would assemble: politicians, heads of state, the remaining crowned heads of Europe, and all the personal friends of the bride and bridegroom. Along the processional route gathered the tens of thousands of ordinary people wearing funny hats and broad smiles and cheering their hearts out. And the streets of London, with their old and new landmarks, were decorated with flags and bunting and good wishes. I suppose subconsciously I was recalling the small boy of 1934 in Edinburgh who listened to a story, and heard about places he had never seen.

*An informal moment with the bridesmaids at Buckingham Palace after
the wedding ceremony. One of the memories Tom Fleming
treasures is little Clementine Hambro gazing adoringly
at her former kindergarten teacher.*

Suddenly St Paul's was filling. In the front row of the bride's guests, were her flatmates from the Old Brompton Road. Among the Prince's guests sat Harry Secombe, Michael Bentine and Spike Milligan. The King of Tonga sat in a chair which he had made himself. (It was twice the width of the chairs for lesser mortals.) Once the processions began, the streets between The Mall and Ludgate Hill were soon echoing to the sound of 800 clattering hooves. The Queen's procession, with its Sovereign's Escort, was half-way along the Strand when the bridegroom's procession, also with Escort, left Buckingham Palace. Five minutes after his departure, the Glass Coach slowly emerged from the garden gates of Clarence House giving us a first glimpse of the exquisitely beautiful bride. We followed the progress of the three processions as they chased each other along the road to St Paul's. Sir John Miller's timing had been immaculate. The bride, with her Escort of Mounted Police, arrived five minutes precisely after her husband-to-be.

I suppose of all the rich memories of that day I treasure the sight of little Clementine Hambro, at five years old the youngest of the five bridesmaids, carrying a posy and with a garland of flowers in her hair, gazing adoringly at her former kindergarten teacher Lady Diana; or the bride's arrival at the Great West Door, as the trumpets sounded, and her immensely long train covered the twenty-two steps of St Paul's; the look bride and groom exchanged as they first stood side by side; the medieval cheers that came from the crowds outside as the Archbishop pronounced them man and wife; the lilting Welsh voice of Mr Speaker (then George Thomas, MP) as he read the lesson; the truly magnificent music; the solicitous glances of The Queen Mother as the granddaughter of one of her closest friends knelt, veiled, beside her own grandson; the curtsy to Her Majesty The Queen, as the bride passed her Sovereign for the first time as Her Royal Highness The Princess of Wales; the smiles of husband and wife as they walked through the congregation of friends and guests; the upward glance at the west gallery that sent the commentary box into a flutter. Then there were the cheers outside, and the old bells of St Paul's pealing over the city, rung by a consultant gynaecologist, a schoolteacher, a

'*Thank goodness it's over.*' *The end of a long day.*
(From left to right)
Top row: *Prince Andrew, Prince Edward, the Princess of Wales,*
the Prince of Wales, Lord Nicholas Windsor.
Bottom row: *Edward Van Cutsem, Clementine Hambro,*
Catherine Cameron, India Hicks, Sarah Jane Gaselee,
Lady Sarah Armstrong-Jones

computer sales manager, an airline pilot and an industrial chemist! The ride back to the Palace culminated in more cheers, from 300 disabled children in the quadrangle (1981 was the International Year of Disabled People) and, in what seemed just minutes, The Mall was a sea of happy faces as thousands walked in an orderly throng towards the Palace railings. Several balcony appearances later the Prince of Wales kissed his Princess, and the roar from the crowd below sent the pelicans in St James's Park into orbit.

At the Palace, the official group photographs were taken, and were followed by a wedding breakfast. At St Paul's, the equipment was already being de-rigged, and that limousine came into its own again as I was rushed, accompanied by two 'strong men', to the commentary position at the Victoria Memorial (the 'Wedding Cake' to generations of BBC commentators) in front of Buckingham Palace. The 'strong men' were normally employed by pop groups to get them through mobs of adoring fans. They had, on this occasion, to get a snap-and-crackle commentator through cheerful crowds who had got there first. They were wonderful. Suddenly, I was on the steps of the Memorial with a Coke and a ham roll. Everybody else had gone to lunch!

We were on the air again by 4 p.m. as the Prince and Princess left Buckingham Palace in an open carriage for Waterloo Station. The entire Royal Family followed into the forecourt waving them off. The royal brothers, Prince Andrew and Prince Edward, who had earlier in the day been the bridegroom's 'supporters', had tied a placard saying 'Just Married' to the rear of the carriage and had also attached inflatable silver hearts which bounced above the couple's heads as they travelled along Parliament Street to Westminster. On the platform at Waterloo the Princess, wearing a coral-pink silk dress and a saucy little straw tricorn trimmed with feathers, gave a farewell kiss to the Lord Chamberlain, Lord 'Chips' Maclean, and to his Comptroller Sir 'Johnnie' Johnston, the two men most responsible for the meticulous planning of the whole day. The name of the engine and destination were the same: 'Broadlands', home of the man Prince Charles had once called his honorary grandfather, the late Earl Mountbatten of Burma.

Alex Thomas and I walked through Green Park to Piccadilly

A cameraman films the Royal Family on the balcony of Buckingham Palace from the Victoria Memorial.

The Prince and Princess of Wales aboard the royal yacht Britannia, *at the start of their honeymoon cruise.*

carrying three large video tapes and our brief-cases. We eventually managed to hail a cab, and got to the Television Centre about 6 p.m. I was despatched, somewhat dishevelled, into a studio to be interviewed by Angela Rippon, and then the process of editing five hours of recording into a sixty-minute 'highlights' programme gathered momentum.

By 10.30 p.m. I was free. There were about a hundred members of staff waiting for taxis to take them home. So I walked over to White City and, still in my morning dress, caught a Central Line train into the West End. In some ways it was a perfect ending. A single ticket back to the world of reality. I had just had the enormous privilege of sharing the sights of a most happy day with 750 million fellow human beings and, into the bargain, been present at what for two delightful, friendly and thoughtful young people had been, as Dr Runcie put it so felicitously in St Paul's, not the end of a fairy tale, but 'the beginning of an adventure'.

THE RECENT
ROYAL TOURS

JOHN OSMAN

The 1947 royal visit to South Africa, described by Frank Gillard in an earlier chapter, was separated by nearly forty years from Her Majesty The Queen's 1986 tour of China. By then many aspects of a royal tour, and of British royalty, had changed.

The tour to China was the first to that country by a British monarch and the coverage of the visit by the media was extensive. The tour included trips to the Great Wall, the Forbidden City and the Terracotta Army. It seemed that at last China was opening its borders to Westerners.

BBC journalist, John Osman, was Diplomatic and Court Correspondent for BBC Radio News at this time. He had already worked in one hundred or so countries and covered royal tours in many parts of the world. He reflects on Her Majesty The Queen's visit to China and on the way the royal tours have changed.

HER MAJESTY THE QUEEN has emerged over the years as a well loved and highly respected figure. Wherever she has been, wherever she still goes (and she's the most travelled British monarch of all time), crowds have flocked, and still flock, to catch a glimpse of her. The younger and newer members of the British Royal Family, beautiful princesses and charming princes, possess their crowd appeal, and indeed their sex appeal; and they attract their substantial quota of television and radio publicity and of newspaper headlines. But, in my couple of score years as a reporter, including four years as BBC Radio's Court and Commonwealth Correspondent, there's been nothing to match the consistent star quality of The Queen; nothing on the constitutional, political or popular scale which can compare with public interest in her alone. I've travelled thousands of miles watching her at work – from China to the Caribbean, Africa to Mexico, India to Canada, America to Zanzibar – and her natural niceness as well as her dedication to duty come shining through. The pledge which she made on her first official overseas trip, in those far-off days in South Africa, she has impeccably fulfilled.

It's no light thing to devote oneself publicly, on one's twenty-first birthday, to a lifetime of service to the people; but Princess Elizabeth did make the promise and, as Queen, she honoured it. This is recognised not just in Britain; nor only in the sixteen other countries of which she is Head of State; nor is it limited to the fifty states of the Commonwealth; but it's recognised throughout the world. In fact, The Queen has become an international symbol of enduring, civilised values; and the focus of aspirations by millions of peoples of all races for a better life.

That is precisely why she was invited to China, the ancient 'Middle Kingdom', with its hundreds of millions of people, its mind-boggling problems, its appalling poverty, its magnificent cultural riches, and its (currently) implacable brand of Communism imposed, however

RIGHT: *The Queen and the Duke of Edinburgh on the Great Wall of China during the third day of their visit in 1986.*

precariously, upon layers of civilisation and brutality which have existed side by side in an apparently eternal embrace. For The Queen went to China not just to put the seal of royal approval on the Anglo-Chinese agreement on the future of Hong Kong, important though that undoubtedly was to the Chinese, to Hong Kong, and to Britain itself. Her presence in China added, in Chinese eyes and in the eyes of the world at large, something else: it lent respectability to the Chinese Communist regime. Today, after the June 1989 massacre in Tiananmen Square, that move looks arguable – especially so since the suppression of the Chinese democracy movement led directly to the calling-off of a planned visit to China in September 1989 by The Queen's own son and daughter-in-law, the Prince and Princess of Wales. Open royal acceptability of China in 1986 had equally openly diminished by 1989.

The reason? Official Chinese policies and attitudes had hardened, thus inevitably British royal plans were affected. The Chinese example is not unique: another contemporary illustration was provided in Romania. There, the late dictator, Nicolae Ceauşescu, had been (back in the 1970s) the first Communist head of state and party leader to be invited to stay in Buckingham Palace during a state visit. But just before he was killed by his own army during December 1989, he was stripped of the knighthood which The Queen had earlier bestowed upon him. Royal actions in such affairs – in China, Romania, or wherever – are pursued on ministerial advice, possibly from Number 10, Downing Street in these two cases, certainly from the Foreign and Commonwealth Office. Equally certainly The Queen would have received the counsel of her own highly efficient and remarkably well informed circle of personal household staff, guided by her Private Secretary, Sir William Heseltine. 'Bill', as The Queen calls him, is an impressively wise yet puckishly quick-witted servant of the monarch. During the Chinese tour, I remember, The Queen was looking at some carpets in Shanghai when a journalist asked her if she was thinking of buying one. 'I might,' she replied, and the journalist then somewhat cheekily asked her if she would use an American Express card. It was a query made jokingly, but the dry answer from 'Bill' was even funnier: 'Oh,' he grinned, 'I think the credit would be quite good, don't you?'

*The Queen surrounded by enthusiastic Chinese children
and accompanied by Sir Geoffrey Howe
(then Foreign Secretary) after a concert at
Canton's Children's Palace.*

That brand of understated humour seemed to me to be a hallmark of
the people round The Queen – not at all stuffy or officious, as is
sometimes suggested.

The Chinese tour was undoubtedly the most interesting of the
royal journeys which I reported over the years and, indeed, I felt so

strongly that nothing could cap it, that at the end of the trip I resigned from the news staff of the BBC. I chose to make it my farewell assignment overseas as I thought it was a good experience on which to quit a lifetime of reporting. Apart from the historic nature of the tour and its important political overtones, the sheer pace, colour and variety of the royal progress were all breath-taking. It added up to an unforgettable pageant of exotic and timeless impressions: the Great Wall of China; the Forbidden City of the Emperors; the Ming tombs; the Horsemen and Warrior columns of statues in Xian; a Buddhist temple in deepest south-west China near Burma; rice fields in Kunming; sailing down the Yangtse; the overwhelming mass of humanity in cities like Shanghai and Canton; and the incredible Chinese food, even at official banquets (ever tried a sea slug?). The tour was also exhausting: early morning 'plane departures to reach another far-flung part of the country; battling with sometimes difficult broad-casting links to London from remote corners; permanent awareness of the near-impossibility of establishing genuine understanding with the Chinese themselves (simply because of one's own lack of any Chinese tongue); and, of course, the sheer slog of the job itself, working well into the early hours of the next morning before getting up a couple of hours later to begin the same incredible round all over again. In short, covering a royal tour these days is a game for a young man or woman; it's not for the likes of sixty-year-olds! Still, I'm glad I did it.

During the tour, Sir William Heseltine's Shanghai joke about royal credit came as no surprise to my ear because, years earlier, I'd already been given cause to appreciate his sense of fun. When, for example, I was re-posted after three years as Moscow Correspondent for the BBC to take up new duties, in 1983, as the Diplomatic and Court Correspondent, I was at Buckingham Palace on my first day in my fresh assignment when I ran into Sir William, then Deputy Private Secretary, in a scarlet-carpeted corridor. He'd met me previously in Africa, on a royal tour, and he asked me how I thought I was going to enjoy my new job. 'Well,' I said, 'I don't really know yet, but I imagine it will be a bit of a change from covering the Kremlin.' He laughed and responded, 'I shouldn't be so certain about that if I were you!' This tickled me; I felt I knew exactly what he meant, even if only because, in its curious way, the sense of protocol in Moscow had hierarchical gradations instantly recognisable at the Court of St James.

But Royal Household humour of this type, spontaneous and unscripted, is not something which members of the Royal Family can easily indulge in – at least publicly. The fact that they do nevertheless crack quite lively and telling jokes, often with an element of royal self-deprecation, is a tribute to their skill at public relations. This generally comes with age and, sometimes, all-too-bitter experience.

For humour can be dangerous if it's slightly off-colour. The Duke of Edinburgh, Prince Philip, is only too aware of this, because, although he's always had something of a gift for informal and 'off-the-cuff' remarks, he's also been known to strike too tasteless a note. Such was the case in China in 1986 when The Queen's Press Secretary, willy-nilly found himself compelled to stress that it was 'grotesque and absurd' to suggest that the Prince had insulted the Chinese people in any way. This came after a British student in China had disclosed to a reporter that the Prince had told him: 'If you stay here much longer you'll go back with slitty eyes.' The royal remarks were described by *The Times* as 'crass'. It was all rather bad luck on Prince Philip, since he was only trying to chat amiably with the young man, and even after his thirty-nine years (then) as The Queen's Consort, not to mention painful familiarity with the methods of Fleet Street, he might not have realised that his remarks would almost certainly be picked up and publicised. Indeed, his Chinese hosts and the Chinese mass media did not notice the incident – at least not until we more implacable British news-hounds had got onto it and tabloid headlines shouted things like 'The Great Wally of China'. The Prince was subsequently rueful and no great damage was done to Anglo-Chinese relations, but the affair emphasised the care with which royalty must choose its words.

In contrast, though, to that episode (which Prince Philip himself would almost certainly describe as 'dropping a clanger') his habit of unleashing a wisecrack can be brilliantly successful. One such example, when he eased what might have been a highly embarrassing moment, came during the independence ceremonies in Kenya. At the climactic moment, the new state's flag, rising up the pole, got stuck. Prince Philip turned to President Jomo Kenyatta and asked: 'Changed your mind?' Everybody found it funny because it eased awkward tension.

In her public statements, it's noticeable how The Queen has schooled herself to be restrained in her humour. She did permit herself a public joke, I recall, in 1972, when she and Prince Philip celebrated their silver wedding. She produced gales of laughter from her audience at a festive luncheon when she began by saying she was sure that everybody would understand why, on that day of all days, she was starting her speech with the words, 'My husband and I'. It was, of course, a phrase which she'd employed hundreds of times all over the world, to the point of it being parodied by television comics. Her own little royal quip about the four words hit the necessary spot in the hearts of the people.

Apart from mere joking, The Queen is limited by the British constitutional nature of things in what she can safely or judiciously say in public. Thus she's never given a real interview to any journalist in her life, though in 1985 she came near to it on the fortieth anniversary of the end of the Second World War in Europe. For the first time, she publicly recalled her memories of Victory in Europe Day in 1945 when she was in the ATS (Auxiliary Territorial Service) and was allowed discreetly to leave Buckingham Palace, in her uniform, to join the crowds outside. She gave her own account of it to one of my distinguished predecessors as BBC Court Correspondent, the author Godfrey Talbot.

A number of attempts has been made over the years to persuade her to give an interview, and I was present on one such occasion. It was in Jamaica, at a royal reception for correspondents and cameramen at the start of a long royal tour. *Time* magazine of America was producing what its publishers call a 'cover issue' devoted to royalty, and a *Time* correspondent had been instructed by his editor to ask The Queen personally for an interview. He was told by royal advisers (let alone other, competing, reporters) that any approach would be useless but, good professional as he was, when his turn came to be presented to The Queen, he made his bid. He quietly explained the *Time* project, acknowledged that he knew that she'd never given an interview, then added – with what he hoped would be a winning smile – 'There has to be a first time, Ma'am'. It was a good performance, but it was matched by The Queen's. With some amusement I remember her resorting to the royal plural in refusing such a brazenly republican request. Smiling just as winningly as the reporter, but knowing that her reply would be unwelcome, The Queen answered 'We never give interviews; but Philip sometimes does.' So *Time*, I think I recall, interviewed Prince Philip.

These receptions given by The Queen for journalists and cameramen accompanying her on a royal tour can be unusual affairs because, for some inexplicable reason, the most hardened veterans of war reporting, revolution, riot, terrorism and international mayhem — men and women toughened by the years – appear frequently to be nervous when faced for the first time with the prospect of meeting The Queen. I know I was in 1979. For some thirty or more years I'd been knocking around the world as a reporter, first for the *Daily Telegraph*, then for the BBC; and at that time I was BBC Africa Correspondent and chairman of the East Africa Foreign Correspondents' Association. As such, I was attending a royal reception in Zambia, with The Queen and Prince Philip standing at the door to welcome their guests, then mingling with them. The moment The Queen walked into the room, and before I'd even had time to seize a whisky, I was taken by the elbow by a Palace official and presented to The Queen – while I was still wondering how to avoid committing any breach of the social code or appearing stupid. The Queen, expert at putting people at their ease, asked all the right questions and everything was fine.

Over the years since, I've been a royal guest in various parts of the world and I came to enjoy the privilege of receiving a royal invitation. But it was always impossible not to remain alert, for The Queen, a true working monarch, has an inquiring mind and uses it. I shall never forget the moment when after my transfer by the BBC from Moscow to be Court Correspondent, I was at the first royal reception of the first tour of my new assignment. Yuri Andropov had just succeeded Leonid Brezhnev as Soviet leader (my last major 'story' as Moscow Correspondent). The Queen's opening words to me after I'd been presented were (without any preliminaries or beating about the bush): 'Tell me about Mr Andropov.' For several minutes I felt I was at a de-briefing by the Director-General of the BBC, only more so! My contribution, I imagine, was pretty minor, because The Queen receives all important state papers including significant ambassadorial messages, and the amplitude of Foreign Office reporting, even distilled through the Foreign Secretary, would have outweighed a reporter's impressions. Nevertheless, it was flattering, if somewhat disconcerting, to be asked by The Queen what I thought about Russia. I'm sure that thousands of people around the world, when they've been asked about their jobs and what they think about things, by The Queen or by one of her family, have felt just the same. It's good for the ego but it's necessary to be on one's toes!

Being light on one's toes is in fact a basic requirement for all who go on royal tours, including members of the Royal Household itself. The household staff, like correspondents and cameramen accompanying the royal travellers, must always be close at hand to fulfil their duties but, unlike we media folk (who are permitted a degree of sartorial laxness according to operational conditions), members of the household have the additional obligation to be properly turned out on all occasions. This often necessitates quick-change acts worthy of any cabaret behind the scenes, with ladies-in-waiting changing their hats and dresses in mid-air on the royal flight between one public engagement and another; and with equerries buckling on, or unbuckling, swords and sheaths, and changing uniforms, according to the degree of formal ceremony awaiting them at the next function. Wardrobe manipulation of a high order is very much part of a royal progress,

The Princess of Wales rubs noses with seventeen-year-old Dawn
Petley in a traditional Maori welcome. Dawn said afterwards
'She needs more practice'.

just as it is of any Paris fashion show, though the garments on display are usually somewhat more orthodox than those draped on models. Dress for each occasion is laid down firmly in a 'little blue book' produced for each and every royal tour.

Whatever the conditions – tropical heat in Africa or Asia, cool rain in Canada or other northern climes – the ladies-in-waiting and the equerries always seemed to me to be impressively adaptable. I learned to respect their resourcefulness over the years. For instance, what does a lady-in-waiting do when her arms are already full of bouquets and posies which her royal boss has passed onto her, and when the boss is about to be given yet more floral tributes? The lady-in-waiting, with no more room in her arms for flowers, can't just gracelessly dump or discard the offerings. One inspired response which I witnessed in Belize was provided by one of The Queen's regular ladies-in-waiting who, overburdened with flowers, summoned a nearby British sergeant-major to her aid and, with an irresistible smile, handed to him her great pile of blossoms and greenery. The sergeant-major, ramrod straight, gallantly accepted the posies before the delighted gaze of assembled ranks of soldiers who, to a man, were unfamiliar with the spectacle of a sergeant-major looking something like a Morris dancer.

The longest royal tours I ever covered were a month's journeying in 1979 around Africa with The Queen, Prince Philip and Prince Andrew (Kenya, Tanzania, Zanzibar, Malawi, Botswana and Zambia); and a six-week trip in 1983 with The Queen and Prince Philip in Jamaica, the Cayman Islands, and up the west coasts of Mexico, the United States and Canada. On such extended tours, with chartered planes sometimes employed to land on bush airstrips in out-of-the-way areas, the physical endurance of writers, photographers and broadcasters in variable weather conditions was sometimes tested to the limit. So a special word of thanks is due to the Medical Officer who, in most of my time reporting royal tours, travelled abroad with The Queen and who was always kind to correspondents and cameramen in need: the then Surgeon-Captain Norman Blacklock. He helped us with problems ranging from upset stomachs to (in one case) setting a broken arm for an ITN reporter.

The Queen and the Duke of Edinburgh escorted by a flotilla of canoes during their visit to the South Pacific Island of Tuvalu.

To a considerable degree, a royal progress nowadays has become something of a television 'spectacular'. The stunning settings from faraway places provide unforgettably romantic images: palm-fringed islands; endless deserts; teeming cities, both ancient and modern, packed with welcoming crowds; lush jungles; towering mountains; wild sea coasts; and enduring architectural wonders like the Taj Mahal in India. Every host country, even if firmly republican, wants to provide a 'royal' welcome for British royalty.

But it's not all glamour and fun on a royal tour. Tremendous care is taken to ensure that royal programmes pay positive attention to what's being done to help deal with often appalling economic and social problems, with royal emphasis being placed on encouragement rather than despair. Efforts are made for the royal visitor to meet ordinary people and not just bigwigs. Thus, we've witnessed the development of the 'royal walk-about' in crowds of sometimes quite frightening size, with most of the people anxious at least to see, and if possible speak to The Queen or one of her family. We've experienced, too, television pictures which are far from romantic but which are just as unforgettable as the sightseeing 'musts' or the glittering, set-piece state occasion. For example, we've viewed The Princess Royal in the slums of Calcutta and Bangladesh, and in African famine zones – a conscientious President for over twenty years of the Save the Children Fund. We've watched the Princess of Wales shaking hands with children suffering from leprosy or from AIDS, and campaigning against drug addiction. For years we've watched Prince Philip ever keen to study something new: technological progress in Silicon Valley in California; rice-growing methods in Chinese paddy-fields; turtle conservation in the Caribbean. The list is endless and impressive.

In its unblinking way, the television camera has also shown us, sometimes, unexpected aspects of royal tours and of royal stage-management. Two incidents immediately come to mind from my own reporting years: one, a scene in Shanghai in 1986 when The Queen's Press Secretary of the time had an altercation with Chinese security officers; and the other, the scene on board *Britannia*, docked at Nassau, during the Commonwealth Conference in the Bahamas in 1985, when a number of The Queen's prime ministers and Commonwealth heads of government turned up late for dinner. They'd been on a boat trip arranged by the Bahamian Prime Minister and the weather had turned choppy so they were delayed. That was the reason advanced. So their hostess, the Head of the Commonwealth (not to mention her other important presidential and prime ministerial guests) was kept waiting. I shan't forget the sight of The Queen's white-gloved fingers tapping impatiently on the polished wooden rail of *Britannia*, as she wondered where a significant group of her guests had got to; nor shall I forget the determined, but perhaps slightly uneasy smile, on the face of the Commonwealth Secretary General as he performed the task of

During a visit to New York the Princess of Wales visits Harlem Hospital's special paediatric unit where she met a baby suffering from Aids. Royal emphasis is placed on encouragement rather than despair.

apologising for the unpunctuality of those messing about in boats other than the royal yacht. The Queen was charming but businesslike; she immediately marshalled the politician-mariners into place, so that, belatedly, the formal portrait of Commonwealth leaders could be taken with the Head of the Commonwealth smiling radiantly in the middle of them – and so that the meal shouldn't get any colder! Television captured most of this episode, unwelcome for the politicians embarrassingly involved.

In the other incident, in Shanghai, I felt rather sorry for the victim of the television lens, Mr Michael Shea (then Press Secretary to The Queen), because when he ran into trouble he was trying to help television crews get their pictures. In the process, he came up against some uncomprehending or over-zealous Chinese security men who were less than helpful, and the result of Mr Shea's attempt to try to assist television was to figure himself on television in what looked like an undignified row.

Security, in an age of international terrorism, is a profound problem for those whose duty it is to protect the Royal Family. Like television, terrorism with a capital 'T' has become a world-wide instrument of persuasion but, unlike television, it's difficult to switch terrorism off. Thus massive security measures are imposed during royal tours when the host authorities have been presented with direct or indirect threats to the safety of their honoured guests. Such security screens tend by their very nature to be heavy-handed and attract attention, some comment inevitably being adverse. But what's the alternative? British police officers of the royal protection team, working closely with the police of the country being visited (and well in advance of the royal visit), normally do their best to be unobtrusive just as they try their hardest to negate any security risk but, in the final resort, the safety of the royal guest is the responsibility of the host state. This does not lessen the burden for British security officials, and one senior officer once remarked pensively to me on an overseas tour that he knew he would never die from ulcer trouble. Puzzled, I asked him why. His reply was that if he'd been destined to end his days through ulcers he'd have been dead long ago!

Now and again, the security problem can be so worrying that public queries are raised as to whether or not a scheduled royal visit should actually proceed; and discreet political decisions have to be taken. Two such occasions come to mind: The Queen's visit to Zambia in 1979 when, because of UDI (Unilateral Declaration of Independence) in neighbouring Rhodesia, fears were expressed about security in the tense Zambian capital of Lusaka; and, five years later, in Jordan. On the eve of The Queen's arrival in Amman, a bomb exploded there outside the hotel where we journalists were all staying, thus guaranteeing maximum publicity. It was apparently the work of a Palestinian pro-Syrian group hostile to King Hussein of Jordan; and it appeared to be an attempt to embarrass King Hussein by getting The Queen's visit called off. The plan failed, but it caused headaches to those whose task it was to advise The Queen to go ahead or not, and whose careers would have been brought to an abrupt end if their advice had been wrong. I recall that in that particular case it was not only the British Ambassador to Jordan who urged The Queen to carry on as usual but that, at the prime minister's country home, Chequers, the Prime Minister, Mrs Margaret Thatcher, the Foreign Secretary and the Defence Secretary were all involved in late night consultations. The ultimate decision always rests with The Queen herself and, true to her sense of duty, she's never been known to shirk a tricky decision.

During her reign she lost her beloved 'Uncle Dickie', Earl Mountbatten, who was murdered in 1979 by Irish terrorists; her daughter, Princess Anne, escaped injury when in 1974 she was attacked in a kidnap attempt in The Mall; and there was a shake-up in the security system of Buckingham Palace itself when in 1982 an intruder called Michael Fagan got as far as The Queen's bedside. The nation shivered, too, when during a ceremony of Trooping the Colour, a young man fired six blank cartridges. The Queen, though, has always insisted on openness: on seeing the people and being seen by them. It's simply not her style to be driven around at high speed in armour-plated vehicles behind dark windows. She and her family accept the risk of assassination or injury as an occupational hazard. I can hear now the roar of appreciation from an American crowd in the state capital of California, Sacramento, in 1983, when The Queen appeared with the Governor on the balcony of the State Capitol. The Governor ushered his royal guest into a position behind a large bullet-proof glass screen. Politely, The Queen paused and waved to the crowd from there. Then, just as politely but quite determinedly, she walked along the balcony to wave to the people from a spot where she could be more plainly seen – and where there was no protection. The gesture was immediately recognised and applauded. The host government was, not unnaturally, taking seriously its responsibility for the security of the royal guest. But the west coast tour did not just provide memories of the rigorous security measures, it was also bedevilled by

The royal yacht Britannia *is a home, an office and provides accommodation for members of the Royal Family and the Royal Household when on tour.*

problems, including the arrival of fierce storms sweeping the California coast. These were so violent that the royal programme had to be altered while *Britannia* battled her way through heavy seas up to San Francisco to take the royal party on board once again.

Named and launched by The Queen in the year of her Coronation,

Britannia, too, is another essential part of the royal scene. Built to replace the fifty-year-old royal yacht *Victoria and Albert*, which was then no longer seaworthy, *Britannia* was designed for two functions: first, as the royal yacht in peacetime, serving as an official and private residence for The Queen and for members of the Royal Family when engaged on visits overseas or voyaging in home waters; and, secondly, being capable of conversion into a hospital ship in time of war. The main reception rooms can be converted into wards to accommodate up to 235 patients.

The royal apartments are in the aft part of the yacht, and contain furniture and other articles from previous royal yachts, including the *Victoria and Albert*. Also in that area is office and cabin accommodation for members of the Royal Household, officials and staff. The Queen and the Duke of Edinburgh took a personal interest in the interior decorations, the choice of furnishings and the general fitting-out. As an independent command, the royal yacht (commissioned into the Royal Navy in January 1954) is administered and commanded by the Flag Officer Royal Yachts. *Britannia*'s crew numbers twenty-two officers and 254 royal yachtsmen, including the Royal Marines Band. Traditions on board include the wearing by junior yachtsmen of an old-fashioned style of uniform with a black silk bow at the back of the trousers, white badges on everyday uniforms instead of the red ones customary in the Royal Navy, and the wearing of white plimsolls rather than shoes. Orders on the upper deck are executed, so far as possible, without spoken words or commands; and by long tradition the customary naval mark of respect of piping the side is normally paid only to The Queen.

No one with the slightest hint of maritime feeling who's ever seen *Britannia* sailing majestically into harbour with the Royal Standard and the White Ensign extended in the breeze, would regret the tax-payers' money spent on her. She immediately conjures up Britain's splendid seafaring past, and the Band of the Royal Marines, with stirring quayside floodlit performances, never fails to send crowds wild with pleasure. It's all so British. I imagine, too, that the hundreds of refugees, including Russians, who were evacuated with British

The Duke and Duchess of York visit Mauritius in 1987.

subjects in 1986 from Aden, when serious fighting broke out in the People's Democratic Republic of Yemen, were even happier than most welcoming crowds when they saw *Britannia* coming round Steamer Point to rescue them! She'd been on her way to New Zealand, for yet another royal visit in her forty-three-year career, when she was diverted to more urgent duties. The Queen and the world approved.

FROM COMMENTARY
TO COMMENT

HELEN HOLMES

The wedding of Her Majesty The Queen's second son Prince Andrew to Miss Sarah Ferguson took place in Westminster Abbey on 23 July 1986. The bride, Miss Sarah Ferguson, was the daughter of Major Ronald Ferguson, a cavalry officer and distinguished polo player, and Mrs Hector Barrantes. It was a smaller wedding than that of Their Royal Highnesses The Prince and Princess of Wales, but nevertheless it reached an estimated world-wide audience of 400 million people through the medium of television. Mrs Helen Holmes was the researcher whose role it was to compile notes, biographies, history and ceremonial details for all the television commentators; it was a task she found illuminating, frenetic and great fun.

> 'It is with great pleasure that The Queen and the Duke of Edinburgh announce the betrothal of their beloved son Prince Andrew and Miss Sarah Ferguson...'

NOTHER ROYAL WEDDING. After months of speculation in the papers, with one girl's name after another linked to Prince Andrew, here was the official news. Now I knew that there was a massive television programme to research and, as it was my third royal wedding, I knew what had to be done. What I should wear was a more difficult problem. However, my dress turned out to be the easy decision this time because a quiet revolution was under way in the BBC coverage of these major events and being in the commentary box gave me a place at the heart of it.

When I first joined BBC Television Outside Broadcasts in a temporary role in 1966, the World Cup football matches were being played out in England. From that passing affair with Sport grew my deep love of Events, the sister department. At that time, a quarter of a century ago, the BBC's proud achievement was summed up in the announcement at the beginning of the programmes, 'We bring you live pictures...' The events had started again after the Second World War with the Coronation coverage, and by 1986 when that young Queen had become a grandmother and the younger members of her family were marrying, the presence of television with its all-seeing cameras and its intrusive lighting was taken for granted by participants and public alike.

Alongside the live pictures are the words of the commentary, and the best commentary of all is the one which the viewer does himself at home. He will never complain about that one! It tells him just what he wants to know and gives him time to put in his own comments. In order to do that he needs some basic facts about what will happen before it actually occurs. He needs to know why the action occurs and then, when the pictures appear on his television screen, he is as well informed as any participant. He feels that he is there and taking part.

Over the long years of building up BBC outside broadcast technique, which now carries with it the prestige and quality associated with televised national events, every producer and commentator has discovered that there is no substitute for detailed and painstaking preparation. On royal occasions, every movement along the processional route has to be known well in advance, gradually building up an understanding of why the action is taking place and thinking how best to show it in pictures and to weave in the words of the story. The positioning of the cameras is crucial. The breathtaking shot that the producer and cameraman find in an event can only occur if the producer has thought carefully about what will happen; where and what the camera will be able to see. The fleeting expression on a face is caught by a quick cameraman, but the fact that he can see it at all is due to the forethought of the producer, and the fact that people at home can see it is due to the engineer. Engineers are immediately involved in the planning. Their ability to rig equipment in unobtrusive and inaccessible places, to provide sensitive lighting and to get the signals to the transmitters make them vital partners in the production team that brings the event to the viewers at home. For the massive coverage of the Investiture of the Prince of Wales in 1969, eighteen months' planning was needed. A royal wedding is just as complicated and just as fraught with logistical problems, but for this wedding in 1986 there were to be only three months for planning. This was the first of two major changes that faced the BBC production team.

Fergie, as we all quickly began to call her, had decided to have a summer wedding like Diana her friend and sister-in-law before her, not the November wedding which would follow the usual pattern of a six-month engagement. The last royal bride to follow that pattern had been Princess Anne, married in Westminster Abbey in November 1972. Fergie, with years of freedom of choice behind her (denied by birth to Prince Andrew), probably little knew what her decision meant to all those involved in arranging a royal wedding. The military staff have to bring back soldiers from abroad and from postings around the world to act as street-liners, escorts and guards of honour; the couturier/design industry has to dress the society world in a few weeks; the Royal Mews, in order to use all their cars and most of their carriages, has to find the horsepower to pull them and the manpower to overhaul them; the royal gardeners and florists have little time to grow or force the number of blooms and plants required for decoration; the police have to fit a crowd control operation into the

*Miss Sarah Ferguson on her way to Westminster Abbey for her
wedding to Prince Andrew on 23 July 1986. She travelled in the Glass Coach
that had been used by The Queen, Princess Alexandra, Princess Anne and the
Princess of Wales on their wedding days.*

middle of a hectic tourist season in London; and, by no means least,
television has only three months to plan the coverage.

The second decision to affect the production team was taken
when Michael Grade, then Director of Programmes in BBC Television,
urged a new style of coverage for major events. By chance, no senior
producers with predominantly 'Events' experience who had covered
the Prince of Wales's wedding in 1981 were still in the Outside

Broadcasts Department. The way stood open for a new style to be tried, but not by staff grounded through long experience in the basic grammar of 'Events' techniques. The basic technique had been developed gradually, over the thirty years since the Coronation, to bring the atmosphere as well as the actuality to the viewer. The use of wide shots and close-ups, the length of time a shot was held, as well as its composition, the timing within the programme of introducing the various places of interest – all this and much else went towards the fundamental skills that producers learned and practised as they developed their own style and put their personal stamp on a production.

Clearly this technique could not be changed within three months before the wedding, nor was there much wish to do so. Viewers did not feel that they were missing anything by watching the events on television – the audience figures in millions showed that – and the less experienced producers were still feeling their way to mastery of the technique. If changes were to be made as the Director of Programmes wanted, they would have to be made in terms of presentation and in the commentary. The commentary box is usually close to the heart of the event, some distance from the control vehicle where the producer and engineering manager select the cameras and check the quality of picture being transmitted. The only means of communication from the vehicle to the box is by a separate microphone into the commentator's headphones. From these headphones comes the continual sound of the producer talking to the cameramen, directing and lining up the next shot, pacing a panning shot to finish when and where he wants it to. In addition, there is the background sound of the music or words of the event itself, and there is the producer's assistant telling the cameramen which will be the next camera to go on air. All this makes a powerful distraction, and yet the outside broadcast commentator's own sensitivity has to catch the mood of the event and continue the story smoothly to the viewers with telling phrases. It has long been accepted by experienced broadcasters that the art of the outside broadcast commentary is the most difficult of all broadcasts forms.

If there were to be a totally new presentation, it followed that a new style of presenter must be found. The emphasis was to be not only on the occasion itself but also on the television personality bringing his own views. He had to be able to switch between interview and comment. The name that came to mind was David Dimbleby, with his quick mind and ready tongue that could meet any unexpected situation. In 1986 the new style was to react to pictures rather than interweave them with the story, and also to add comments from people involved in the occasion, sitting in a commentary box just away from the centre of things.

At previous royal weddings the commentary box had always been inside the Abbey or Cathedral and invariably at the top of a wearisome flight of worn stone spiral stairs, often with a ladder for good measure at the top of that. I have no head for heights and I receive much kindness from the production team now that they know, but it was at Canterbury that I first came across the problem.

The commentary position there is normally in the triforium, that space above the ceiling of the side aisles and under the sloping roof, about sixty to seventy feet above the floor. The very word was first coined in Canterbury Cathedral where three arches (the 'tri' part of the word) look out between the pillars high over the nave. I first attended the enthronement of an archbishop when Archbishop Coggan went to Canterbury in 1974 and the point of having the commentary position there was to be able to look down on the altar, presbytery and St Augustine's Chair at the heart of the proceedings. I was walking slowly up the final twist of a spiral staircase following Tom Fleming and the stage manager who were carrying the brief-cases. Suddenly they were not to be seen and I supposed they had gone through the arch straight ahead of me, so I stepped forward. Only then, as I stood rivetted, did I realise how far up we had climbed. In front of me, over a raised stone threshold, was a ledge just over a foot wide, tracing its way round the curving east end at triforium level, about sixty feet above the mosaic floor. Carefully braced against the archway I thought, 'Well, they can't have gone that way', and turned to the safety of the stone walls to look for an opening. Within a few minutes they were back, framed in the archway and apparently standing on air. 'Go that

The television commentary box overlooked Westminster Abbey.
David Dimbleby's chair moved along the rails from the window to
the television screen only making it just in time!

way? Without wings?' The route to the commentary box lay along this narrow ledge, edging between the pillars of the arch and the wall behind and then a sharp right turn, over the stone threshold on to the ceiling above the north choir aisle. With the help of the two stalwarts, one pushing and one pulling, I made it to the commentary area for the rehearsal and I made it back again the next day for the programme. For once my concentration slipped. I kept thinking about the return journey. I have a vague recollection of the Archbishop preaching about walking forward fearlessly – if only he knew!

This time – for Fergie's wedding – it was very different. A portacabin was carefully lowered on to its scaffolding on the far side of Broad Sanctuary diagonally opposite the Abbey's west doors, early one Sunday morning when the traffic was quiet. Only a few wooden steps led up to the door, for the floor was only six feet, not sixty, above the ground. Within the cabin was a pensinsular desk of monitors, microphones and technical equipment, and around the edge was just enough room for our scripts, but not enough room (there never is enough room!) for my notes, for David's cards and for the notes of Sophie Hicks, the fashion reporter who was to comment on the dresses. The end wall was replaced by tinted glass in which was framed the Abbey's great doors and the road from Parliament Square, so that David could see and hear the arrival of everyone from the man who swept the carpet to the Guard of Honour and The Queen herself. David's chair was at the end of six-foot long parallel runners so that he could push it from the desk where he commented to the tiny interview area in front of the glass window, where he talked to people who came to the studio on their way to the wedding. At the far end of the cabin, now effectively a portable studio, were chairs where they could wait. However, the British are more self-conscious about television appearances than the Americans, who are used to this style, and a great deal of coffee was dispensed by calm stage-managers at the other end of the studio.

This ingenious adaptation of a studio meant that the viewer could see exactly where David was and over his shoulder, through the glass, could see all that was happening outside the Abbey while David was talking to his guests. The viewer missed nothing – and yet somehow he did, for it was an unusual feeling of watching the occasion as a member of the crowd, distanced by glass, rather than being at the very heart of it all. The technique is still used in the coverage of the State Opening of Parliament where viewers can see, over David's shoulder, The Queen in her carriage with the clattering horses of the Sovereign's Escort departing from the Palace of Westminster, while the discussion with politicians about the speech from the throne goes on in the studio. So the technique has become comment from a personality, not commentary.

However different the approach on the day, one thing remained certain. Without accurate details and understanding of the occasion all the preparation would be in vain. With only ten weeks to work, instead of the usual six months, the days and evenings would be very full. Like any family arranging a wedding, many of the details were left to the last minute and so no information could be made available to the press; but unlike any other family, there was a wealth of precedent and pageantry, all of which could be researched well before the final details came out. Once again I could pick up the threads of communication with officials who over the years had become friends rather than voices at the end of a telephone.

Now that the presence of television is accepted as inevitable, the help that is so necessary to us is very readily given by those who are almost overwhelmed by the extra work they are called upon to do. One of the first visits is always to the scene of the event, and this meant a warm welcome from the vergers at Westminster Abbey. Since we had last been there for a royal wedding thirteen years before, when Princess Anne had been married, there was now a woman Verger on the staff, the first in the 900-and-more years of the Abbey's history. Maureen Jupp's ready smile and deep love of the place showed how much a part of the team she had already become. The team of vergers led by the Dean's Verger, David Dorey, was still coping with the normal daily flow of thousands of visitors, but when our lights and scaffolding came to be rigged during the weeks before the wedding day, their busy routine was shattered. However, they continued with 'business as usual'. David Dorey sorted out every query with good-humoured patience and on the day carried his Elizabethan silver wand of office before the Dean and his Sovereign to the high altar. It was his cues at the wedding that controlled everyone's movements in the sanctuary, so that clergy and readers arrived in their right positions at the right times.

There is always a quiet peace in that great house of prayer, and I well remember the day of rehearsal when every last-minute check was being made to flowers, candles, brass, carpet, lights, cameras, altar cloths, and many adjustments were needed. I sat beside the Receiver General, Reg Pullen, who was an old hand at these weddings. There was an oasis of calm as he let the others carry out their delegated tasks, answering a question, giving advice when called upon. This was one of his last major services before he retired after a quarter of a century working as Surveyor and Administrator in the Abbey. He lived in an ancient house in the cloisters where his wife, herself the daughter of his predecessor, had lived as a little girl. They too had been married at the high altar in the Abbey and their names came in the Register of Marriages immediately after The Queen's marriage entry in 1947, nearly forty years before. I think he was recalling a lot of memories that day.

The Abbey is a treasure-house not just of history and architecture, but of lovely things. One of the 'finds' for us on television when Princess Anne was married was the two pages of marriage vows from a decorated twelfth- or thirteenth-century prayer book. The Librarian came across them in an old chest in the Muniments Room, high up behind the arches that overlook the crossing. 'For better for worse, for richer for poorer, in sickness and in health': I wondered how many couples had used these words in the old Anglo-Saxon measured flow, but in such different conditions. 'To love, honour and obey' had been the words of the old Prayer Book used in 1972 by Princess Anne, but Fergie had chosen the new Alternative Service Book, and with much discussion in the newspapers it was learned that she would not promise to obey.

Those working with her and Prince Andrew, making a BBC film about their engagement and their plans, had been struck by the force of character behind her cheerful spontaneity. Yet we who had looked through the gilded bars of the Palace prison for years had wondered whether she realised how much of her own freedom would be lost when she lived in the spotlight reflected from the Crown. She intended to learn to fly in order to be able to talk with understanding to her husband about his work, but we were not sure whether she would be able to continue her own career against the pressure of royal work, and the resentful cries of others, who thought she succeeded only by her position and not by her merit.

But at this stage Fergie was still surrounded by the ordinary people with whom she had grown up, and there were many ordinary people in the Abbey, too, who were helping in the wedding day preparations: the ushers, the Brotherhood of St Edward, the bell-ringers who rang out the wedding with Stedman Caters and a peal of 5000 changes later on in the day and, by no means least, the flower arrangers. Flowers transformed the Abbey, and my strongest memory of that wedding in 1986 is the gentle perfume of flowers that filled the Abbey in the two days before the wedding. Forty ladies from around Britain, who were members of the National Association of Flower Arrangement Societies, had spent weeks planning displays. Their plans were meticulously sketched out and every arranger received precise details about size, shape, materials and what they had to do from Pam McNichol. Between the arches of the nave, great balls of flowers were suspended. They were made of two joined flower baskets filled with oasis and covered with cling film. Down the front of the twelve columns in the nave were long plaques of flowers and a special stand was built to frame the archway under the organ loft. More than forty-one arrangements hung from the nave through the choir stalls and the sanctuary into St Edward's Chapel behind the altar, and some rose in triumphant towers eleven feet high, framing the royal cypher on the arch of the Confessor's Chapel. The ladies moved in on Sunday – the wedding was to be on Wednesday morning at 11.30 – and for those three days they worked unceasingly. Flowers in buckets of water filled the wide ambulatory around the sanctuary and the Confessor's Chapel. It was the only time that I have seen the Dean's Verger, David Dorey, just a little agitated. In their enthusiasm the ladies climbed to the top of tall ladders, reaching out to fix the elusive bloom that would complete their display. They held on to filigree fretwork over the choir stalls and to pinnacles high in the organ loft which could never have borne their weight if they had slipped. All was well, but at the time it was better not to wonder, and I think the Dean's Verger went to sit quietly in his office and worry.

Time was passing, my telephone never stopped ringing with the answers to my interminable questions, and gradually the jigsaw pattern built up. We had a meeting of the six producers, the engineering managers and the teams to co-ordinate timings and plans. Selina Scott would be at Buckingham Palace in a studio similar to David's, and Mike Smith would be roving down The Mall talking to visitors, not forgetting the two Germans who had won their trip to London as a prize. By now we knew when roads would be closed and what security arrangements the police were making. (Passes galore that changed frequently; don't let it even cross your mind about losing one!) We knew when Major Ferguson would arrive at Clarence House to ride with his daughter. We knew the coachman's name.

The military decisions had been taken, rehearsed in the very early morning and carried out with their dependable precision. The services are always an anchor in moving pageantry when various processions can be on the route simultaneously. There were troops from the three Services along the route and forecourts, all of whom had to be correctly named and described when the time came. Their position on the route was worked out so that the producers knew when to expect to see them as they travelled to their various starting and dispersal points.

Few people know that a different rank of person merits a different level of escort. The Queen clearly has the largest Sovereign's Escort. On this occasion Prince Andrew had a Captain's Escort to and from the Abbey and a smaller Travelling Escort for the departure on the honeymoon. When Miss Sarah Ferguson left Clarence House on the journey that would lead to her becoming the Duchess of York, she had a small Escort of Life Guards by special permission of The Queen, for as a commoner it had been suggested at first that she should be accompanied by the Military Police. In the event, she travelled in the Glass Coach that had been used on their wedding days by The Queen, Princess Alexandra, Princess Anne and the Princess of Wales.

There were five processions to the Abbey that morning and, all told, seven inside it. I see from my jigsaw puzzle of timings that at 10.55 a.m. it was 'processions everywhere' and the commentator had to be prepared to flit from one to another as the cameras spotted them. He needed the correct information about the people, carriages, horses, livery and harness, postillions and escorts. That was only the Royal Mews information. There was the topography of London, not for-

The bride arrives at the Abbey where designer Linda Cierach is on hand to make sure the dress is just right.

getting the Whitehall Theatre which was showing a Rix farce called *When We Are Married*. Notes had to be prepared on the origin and meaning of the wedding service, the details of the bridesmaids' and pages' outfits, biographies of numerous guests and much more. But BBC Television was by no means the only organisation working that weekend, rigging, lighting, asking, typing, planning, checking. The guests had by now replied to the Lord Chamberlain's Office and his staff were arranging the seating in the Abbey. The Diplomatic Corps were seated by the Protocol Department of the Foreign Office, but the main burden of the Abbey seating plan fell on experienced shoulders in St James's Palace. They bravely promised this final information for Monday morning and as on previous occasions they met their target with good humour and tired eyes. Luckily for me they knew everyone and helped with the short biographies on the guests.

When Monday came our own rehearsals were upon us. There was no time for shopping now and I brought out the outfit which I had bought for The Queen's sixtieth birthday programmes but which I had not worn because the weather had been too cold and wet. The lights went up in the Abbey, and from the Choir School we could hear the boys practising. They had cheerfully given up the first three days of their summer holiday to sing at the wedding. During the day the commentators from overseas broadcasting organisations arrived. There were twenty-four different organisations in London and five or six more who received the BBC pictures in their own countries and added their commentary there. In the early evening, after the commentators had had a chance to walk the route and to remind themselves of the size of the Abbey, the main briefing was held.

I had prepared and written a special briefing pack for Commonwealth and overseas broadcasters, partly because their audiences do not have the background knowledge of the occasion that British audiences have, and partly because they look at the event in a different light. It was a chance to meet some old friends, but the majority of commentators were new to me. The Executive Producer, Tim Marshall, explained to them the whereabouts of the cameras, what they could expect to see and the arrangements made for their own commentary booths at Television Centre. Each broadcasting organisation had its own booth with a television and with microphones linked to its own country. The commentator watched the wedding on the television screen and added his commentary in the booth in his own language. With this going on simultaneously in so many different languages, the room sounded like the Tower of Babel.

Then came question time. A sharp-eyed American asked for the definition of the Free Church Federal Council and why the Moderator was there. So, a brief explanation, thinking on my feet of who they were, why they had been created. As I gave the answer to that, it reminded me of a story too detailed to tell there. In 1588, immediately after the failure of the planned invasion by the Spanish Armada from

During the service bridesmaid, Laura Fellowes, had to tell pageboy, Prince William, to behave!

a Catholic country, Queen Elizabeth I had gone to stay with a Catholic family on her journey around England. It demonstrated that the Protestant Queen had no personal doubts about the loyalty of her subjects whatever their religious practice. Four hundred years on, Queen Elizabeth II could demonstrate equally clearly that nonconformists and Catholics have an active part to play in the services which are at the heart of her family's life, or at other occasions which reflect national feelings. Questions and answers, technical and factual, ranged on for two hours against the murmur of instant translation. By the end of that evening I felt that I too had had a main rehearsal. There were invitations for me to appear on overseas broadcasts but there was no time to fit them in while I was so busy at the commentary studio at Westminster.

The Press Centre was now available in the newly-built Queen Elizabeth Conference Centre just behind our studio on Sanctuary Green, and that too showed the tremendous overseas interest that there was in this wedding. Television monitors over every desk and typewriter showed BBC and ITV output and it was easy for the reporters to keep in touch with the event by television as they came from the Press stands to write or 'phone in reports to their newspapers.

The day itself came with an early start, leaving home at six o'clock. David Dimbleby had been broadcasting on breakfast television before I arrived. The last despatch rider was sent to the overseas commentators at Television Centre with details of the wedding dress, still embargoed until the bride was actually seen. Our studio's bustle and movement gave way to quiet tension and the main programme began. For hours there was intense concentration: going down the route camera by camera from the Palace to the Abbey looking at people and places; slotting in interviews in the studio as people arrived, some of them early, none of them late; and the fashion reporter sitting across the desk with the drawing of Fergie's dress at last revealed with its pretty detail. So the hours passed my eyes on the screen, on the script, on the notes; glancing for the next person to be interviewed; procession details to hand; ears atuned to the Producer's camera instructions and aware of the crowds outside chattering and commenting as guests arrived. There was the quick switch from interview to comment, with David's chair moving rapidly on its rails from the window to the television screen, making it only just in time – and that impish smile on his face that showed that he had known just how close it had been.

Finally, that part of the programme was finished. The Duke and Duchess of York were back in the Palace, their balcony appearance over. I wondered if the Duchess had changed to her reserve bouquet, kept in the fridge for freshness, when the photographs were taken. The crowds were thinning round the Victoria Memorial and we moved to the other studio outside the Palace for the honeymoon departure. There was just time for a hasty sandwich and fruit juice as I telephoned the Palace Press Office to learn the menu for the royal lunch:

DICED LOBSTER, EGG AND TOMATO
IN A MORNAY SAUCE

ROAST LAMB
DECORATED WITH TOMATOES

RING MOULD OF SPINACH
FILLED WITH MUSHROOMS

BROAD BEANS

NEW POTATOES

STRAWBERRIES IN WHIPPED CREAM
IN THE FORM OF A CROSS OF ST GEORGE

As the time for the honeymoon departure drew near, we could see the royal children playing in the quadrangle. Finally the orders were given. The first section of the Travelling Escort left the gates and the 1902 State Landau came through the archway with the Royal Family seeing them off. The Queen ran quickly to catch four-year-old Prince William of Wales who could easily have gone on to the forecourt where the horses of the Escort were about to move forward to follow the State Landau. Her officials said later that they had never seen The Queen run before, and had never known her so happy as on that day. The Queen entertained the two families, the royal guests and family friends to lunch yet also kept her eye on details such as getting them all to sign the special royal register brought to the Palace for the occasion.

Prince William was returned to the safety of his father's arms, the rear division of the Travelling Escort swung into position behind the State Landau and we started the last procession of the day to the Royal

*The Duke and Duchess of York travel to the Royal Hospital, Chelsea, where
they left by helicopter for the start of their honeymoon.*

Hospital Chelsea, where a helicopter took the Yorks away from our
cameras. The live programme was over. For the first time for hours
we had a rest until a new commentary was prepared for the edited
version to be broadcast in the evening.

I finally got home at about 9.30 p.m. to hear the telephone ringing
from friends in Hamburg who had enjoyed it all. Next day the telexes
arrived from all around the world – Tokyo, Italy, Australia, Taiwan,
the Commonwealth countries. The pictures had been well received.

When I returned from a brief holiday there was a letter from a
viewer asking for the formula for polishing Churchill's bronze statue
in Parliament Square because the bronze ornaments on her family
tomb needed attention. Beeswax and lanolin was the answer, but the
exact proportions were known only to the workmen who had to do the
job. I had known that even that detail would come in handy one day.

INTO
THE NINETIES –
THE QUEEN MOTHER

GODFREY TALBOT, LVO, OBE

Godfrey Talbot has been writing and broadcasting about Her Majesty Queen Elizabeth The Queen Mother for over forty years. In 1948 he was the first BBC Court Correspondent accredited to Buckingham Palace and has been able to observe the Royal Family at work and at leisure. Consequently, he has acquired a wealth of knowledge about The Queen Mother and a deep respect for this unique lady. He now reflects on those years, as The Queen Mother enters the nineties.

THE LADY OF THIS CHAPTER has been an unforgettable figure in almost all the royal panoramas brought to memory in this book. Today's Queen Elizabeth The Queen Mother, now in her nineties, was a star from the start. Her own life story began with the twentieth century, long before broadcasting. So when the pioneer BBC was first covering royal occasions she was already an adult member of Britain's first family. Now she has become the senior person and loved head of that large clan, the House of Windsor, the best known 'Royal' in the world, long established in the hearts of so many people that the tides of affection surrounding her are unprecedented. No wonder there was such enthusiasm over the celebrations which spread throughout 1990, fore and aft of her actual ninetieth anniversary on 4 August.

The most spectacular event, fully broadcast, was the Ninetieth Birthday Tribute staged on Horse Guards Parade in London on an evening of blazing June sunshine. It was an extravaganza involving march pasts of thousands of men and women of the Armed Forces (Her Majesty is Colonel-in-Chief of many regiments and uniformed corps in Britain and throughout the Commonwealth), massed bands and massed choirs, and a quite extraordinary pageant formed by representatives of very varied civilian organisations of which The Queen Mother is a personally enthusiastic patron. Thus we saw learned doctors and skipping children streaming past in salute, followed by lorry loads of war heroes, famous actors, ambulances and hospital nurses, plus racehorses, dogs and all sorts of farm animals. And, the centre of it all, there was the nonagenarian herself on the reviewing platform, on her feet for a whole hour, waving acknowledgement once a minute as the processions came by. London had never seen anything like it. The whole thing was Trooping the Colour – and much more.

It has been my good fortune to know Her Majesty for very many of her own and broadcasting's years, and to have been professionally present at the great state events and on innumerable royal tours undertaken by herself and by her descendants. Through decade after decade I have been witness to the weaving of the Windsor tapestry. And now, to write a Queen Mother chapter from all this is a pleasure, as it would be to many a seasoned commentator or cameraman, simply because the spell of her unchanging warmth and shine is irresistible, sometimes making dispassionate reporting seem near to adulation.

She was born in 1900, named Lady Elizabeth Angela Marguerite Bowes-Lyon, ninth of ten children of the fourteenth Earl and Countess of Strathmore. She was of an ancient and noble Scots lineage – though a clinical historian would perhaps describe her as a commoner who married into royalty.

She was born in London, but from the very first days of her life her home was the family's country house in Hertfordshire, St Paul's

Walden Bury, not far from Stevenage. In the same breath it has to be said that it was in Scotland, in the Strathmores' great Castle of Glamis, a few miles north of Dundee where foothills of the Grampians begin, that much of Elizabeth's girlhood was spent, early in the century.

Her Majesty has other homes when in 'the Northern Realm' now: Birkhall near Balmoral and her own little Castle of Mey on the northernmost tip of the Highland coast. But historic Glamis, and especially the lively warmth and unassuming work of its close-knit family in the midst of which she grew up, has had an abiding influence on the character of the famous figure she became, the royal lady to whom for the last forty years the world has given the admiring accolade of 'the Queen Mum'.

It would have been fascinating, had there existed even a few feet of 'moving pictures' of the early days, to have been able to glimpse some archive film of that quicksilver child who turned into a carefree but caring young woman. First-hand stories have been told to me of how she was everybody's friend whether dancing into a Glamis village shop, saying, 'Hello, I'm Elizabeth Lyon', or vitalising society gatherings in the old county of Angus.

But there is no such record. It was all long ago; and anyway she was not 'news' then, nor was there television or radio. Even when, in April 1923, she married the King's son, that event was thirteen years before the BBC's pioneer television transmissions started, and as to radio, daily broadcasting had begun only a few months earlier. So we have only 'stills', some set-piece family groups, and just a little ciné film of the bride's journey to Westminster Abbey.

Not that the British Broadcasting Company (it wasn't a 'Corporation' then) failed to attempt its own coverage of the wedding ceremony. But the request to put something of the service on 'the wireless' was turned down flat. The Dean of Westminster had an open mind, but the Chapter at the Abbey were horrified at the idea of direct commentary or any relay of sound from inside the church: in their view it would be intrusion by microphone, and 'disrespectful people might hear the service, perhaps some of them sitting in public houses with their hats on'!

The man Lady Elizabeth married was Prince 'Bertie', the Duke of York, who was the second son of King George V. The wedding made Lady Elizabeth a Duchess and a Royal Highness at twenty-two.

The Duke, a personable but shy and hesitant man, was accustomed to living well outside the limelight of public interest: that light was the one which shone abundantly on the first son, the Prince of Wales, Heir to the Throne; and Bertie was content to be in his 'Prince Charming' brother's shadow. But he was not lacking in purpose and persistence when he fell in love with Elizabeth. This happened on visits to the Strathmores at Glamis after the First World War (during which the Castle had been turned into a convalescent home for wounded soldiers, with the young Bowes-Lyon daughter cheerfully helping her mother in tending the guests).

The Duke's courtship lasted two years. Elizabeth was fond of her suitor, but she had understandable reluctance about the prospect of exchanging the open, relaxed ambience of her family and circle of friends for the restricted and stuffy existence which the first family led in those days. She did not seek royalty for herself or wish to be swallowed by a court which in old King George V and Queen Mary's time was so rigidly conventional as to be almost Victorian – immensely different from the Buckingham Palace of today. But in the end her affection for and admiration of the Prince triumphed. And her 'yes' transformed his life as well as hers (as it was to transform the Palace itself before long). After marriage, the Duke of York had a delightful family life of his own. There was not only his wife, the 'Little Duchess', as newspapers began to call her, but presently there were two lively daughters, Princess Elizabeth and Princess Margaret.

The Duchess accompanied her husband on the official functions and the first long journeys which began to establish her as Britain's best-liked public figure in many parts of the former Empire, now the Commonwealth. Her smile, the ease of manner in which that dignity and infectious laughter combine, the brightness of her clothes and the sparkle of the blue eyes – all those attributes were manifest, to the pleasure of all who met her. And they still are.

Stories that instance her sparkling character have come down

*King George VI and Queen Elizabeth on an official
visit to France. They are watching an official
tableau.*

through the years. There was, I remember, one blazing hot African
morning on which Queen Elizabeth was to review a huge tribal march
past. She appeared, on the open-air dais, wearing a long brocade
evening gown, brilliant jewels, the sash of the Garter and a diamond
tiara. To the raised eyebrow of a lady-in-waiting she explained: 'I must
look the part. These people have travelled great distances for today.
Without these props they might not know it was me.'

She has never been nonplussed. On quite another occasion, in
Africa again, a line of local dignitaries being presented to The King
and herself included an old man who had been a Boer War fighter in
1900 and who had never got over his enmity. He had told his friends

that he was allowing himself to be presented only because he wanted to 'spit into the eyes of the visitors' – which he nearly did when he stood before Queen Elizabeth. What he managed was a scowl and the words: 'I can never forgive what the English did to my country.' Her Majesty neither hesitated nor ceased smiling, though the royal entourage were horrified. She replied straight away, 'Oh I do so understand. We in Scotland often feel the same.' The Boer retreated – not only deflated but converted too. The quick-witted Bowes-Lyon informality had won again.

Her resilience and dependability were to be tested to an extreme degree not many years later, for 1936 brought its bombshell to the Crown and complete revolution in the lives of the York family. It was of course the abdication of Bertie's older brother – 'David', Prince of Wales who had for a brief eleven months been King Edward VIII – which thrust that dismayed and unprepared husband of Elizabeth's upon the throne, precipitated the family into Buckingham Palace, and brought the Duchess to unsought stardom. She became Queen Consort, wife of the man who, however reluctantly, was now reigning King, George VI.

That she was an incomparable support to her husband is a matter of history. The defection of her brother-in-law, Edward VIII ('Duke of Windsor' in his twilight years of exile) might well have wrecked the monarchy. That it did not was in great measure due to Queen Elizabeth's vital role beside the new Sovereign. Her very presence gave him confidence. She devoted some part of every day to help him gradually overcome many of his speech hesitations. As the Coronation of 1937 drew near – it was the ceremony at which she as well as The King were to be crowned – Her Majesty would sit beside him in one of their rooms at the Palace, going through the responses he would have to speak at the Abbey. Although at those personal rehearsals he was wearing one of his usual lounge suits, she encouraged him into the habit of wearing the heavy crown on his head as he spoke the lines.

When at last the Coronation day of 1937 arrived the BBC got into Westminster Abbey for the first time on a state occasion. The

The King and Queen driving through Washington DC in America.
'Yes Mam, the British have recaptured Washington' was the
headline in the newspapers.

microphones of radio were admitted, but none of our television cameras. We had to make do with moments of ciné film. But the processional routes between the Abbey and the Palace, along decorated streets thronged by crowds, were covered 'live' – and were delightedly viewed in their homes by the relatively few families who in those early days possessed television sets. In fact, Coronation day brought the BBC's first ever big outside broadcast of its kind, heroically mounted by a television service barely six months old.

Sterner events were soon clouding the new reign. But in the summer of 1939, only weeks before the Second World War broke out, The King and Queen crossed the Atlantic and carried out a long-planned and very full tour of Canada and the United States. In the spectacular success which their journeys turned out to be, Elizabeth's effect on press and public was paramount. Crowds swarmed to get a view of her, at railway stations and rural halts as well as in the city streets and department stores.

At the World's Fair in New York, I remember, there were times when you couldn't hear the bands' music for the yells of 'Attaboy, Queen!' And in the capital, where President Roosevelt was the host, newspapers summed up Her Majesty's impact with enormous headlines such as: 'Yes Mam, the British have recaptured Washington'.

Frenzied though many of the tour scenes were, the visit had a serious diplomatic purpose: the royal pair were ambassadors. At the time, many Americans had been myopically hugging neutrality and ideas of cosy isolationism, imagining that the Hitler threat to Europe was nothing to do with them. But the British visit, indeed especially The Queen's quiet personal conversations, helped Mr Roosevelt and his advisers to swing a full tide of opinion and of aid towards Britain and the Allies.

When the war came, British people soon realised for themselves that they had a King and Queen who had become professionally assured. Throughout the war years the pair were a recognised focus of national identity and purpose. For those two Palace people 'stayed put', even in the times of greatest peril, after Dunkirk, when we were in unmistakable danger of a German invasion from the sea and the air, and in the Blitz when cities and towns were being pounded by the Luftwaffe's bombs. Buckingham Palace was hit nine times during the raids. One of The Queen's comments, often recalled, was made after the first wrecking of their home (and a narrow escape for herself and The King). 'I'm almost glad. Now I can look the East End in the face.'

Austere though life had become, she did not altogether stop entertaining at the Palace, making sure, however, that the routine restrictions of food and fuel rationing were observed. When Sir John Reith, the man who had built up the BBC, dined there he found that although silver plate was on the table, the fare placed on it was scanty: jellied soup, ham mousse, a bit of cold chicken followed by an ice-cream. Only one small electric fire 'heated' the room.

The King and Queen inspect bomb damage to Buckingham Palace. 'I'm almost glad. Now I can look the East End in the face', she said.

The two Princesses had been packed off to Windsor Castle, thought safer than London. They continued their studies there privately, instructed by a governess and tutors, who in turn were under the guidance of their mother. She, The Queen, was for most of the time in London with her husband, and was often seen in public. In 1940 and 1941, during months when peril to these islands was at a peak and when neutral observers were reporting that Britain might be defeated, Sovereign and Consort were 'never short of advice' when the enemy's invasion forces were poised just across the Channel and descent by grey paratroops on south-east beaches or indeed on London's Mall were a real possibility. There were plenty of counsellors urging the Palace that Queen Elizabeth and the Princesses, at least, should leave the country for the safety of Canada. Her Majesty's answer became legendary: 'The Princesses cannot go without me. I cannot go without The King. The King will never go.' She proceeded to take revolver shooting practice, and announced that if there were an invasion she would join the defenders. Visions that Germans landing on a Kentish shore might find themselves facing a Boadicea in powder-blue were hard to resist!

During my own years as a War Correspondent overseas there were one or two spells when I was called back to the United Kingdom, still on duty. My experiences during those 'breaks' were less note-worthy than reporting the fighting at El Alamein or Cassino and the liberation of northern Europe, but happenings during that home front coverage are just as clear in memory as the fighting in foreign lands. They enabled me to see The King and Queen visiting blitzed towns, air-raid shelters, military hospitals, munitions factories, gun sites, airfields and army camps all over the country.

Security restrictions, necessarily imposed in wartime, prevented our immediate broadcasting of the details of those tours: it could never be reported just where 'the Royals' were at this or that moment, for to do so would have been to provide information of the greatest interest and use to German bombers. But nobody present during the royal visits could forget the morale-boosting atmosphere of them.

There was, for instance, the homesick and usually pretty in-articulate sergeant at a camp which had been established as a base for United States Army troops, a chap who gushed like a girl after Queen Elizabeth had stopped to chat with him. 'Gee, fellers,' he told his buddies, 'that was a swell lady. Talked to me like she was Mom. Was sure interested in every darn thing I said. Yep, even my old man's stomach ulcer.'

The Queen became a rallying point to millions of people opposing Nazi tyranny. There may well have been truth in the reports coming out of German-occupied territories that Hitler had called her 'the most dangerous woman in Europe'.

Soon after Europe was freed and the war ended, my experience

Godfrey Talbot's Press Pass and badge. He was the BBC's *first accredited Crown Correspondent.*

of reporting the Royal Family took an official turn: I became the BBC's first accredited Court Correspondent. It was the start of a quarter of a century in that post, and a quarter of a million miles of royal tours all over the world. The beginning of it all – the travelling and the talking of it all, the years of front seats as well as back stage views – was an afternoon of agreeable surprise. I had been asked by my Director of News to pop down from Broadcasting House to Buckingham Palace to have a word with my 'contact', the Royal Press Secretary of those days, Commander Richard Colville, a courtier of the old style, faithful and protective, polite and punctilious. No one had better manners or better paperwork; but the Commander's style was stiff, to say the least. His crisp way of dealing with seekers of information suggested a built-in opinion that journalists were suspect characters, and that if in your work you went too far beyond the Court Circular you should be on your way to a dungeon in the Tower.

But I needn't have worried on that first day in the Palace. After only a few minutes in Colville's little office I was whisked out of it and abruptly marched down a well-carpeted corridor in the charge of middle-aged Page, in livery of scarlet and gold, who ushered me into a handsome drawing-room with words: 'Mr. Godfrey Talbot, Your Majesties'. I was face to face with Queen Elizabeth, her smile and that well known gesture of outspread hands giving me an immediate welcome. The King joined her almost at once; and then, much to my enjoyment, there ensued a half-hour chat – over the teacups. All very informal, but a private 'audience'. I talked too much and too freely, I think, but that was Her Majesty's natural effect: when she meets you, smiles at you, asks a well-informed opening question, you have the impression that you are the one person in the world she had been wanting to see. But after I came out of the room I realised that I had been led, in the most relaxed way, to *give* information – about myself, my family, my upbringing, my tastes and opinions and experience.

During the immediate years that followed, I was able many times to see how The Queen's personality enlivened special visit programmes which on the face of it were dull routine. At Stratford-upon-Avon, for instance, when the Royal Shakespeare Company put on *King Henry VIII* for the royal pair, The Queen impulsively included in the day's schedule a visit backstage just before the performance. Thus there was a call at the dressing-room of Anthony Quayle, who was playing the lead role: Quayle was already in costume when this encounter took place, and I remember The Queen pointing to his legs and laughing. 'You've got the Garter on all wrong,' she said and, turning to her husband, added, 'You show him.' His Majesty put one foot up on a chair and, pulling at his trouser-leg, took the golden badge and buckled it properly over his own leg (over his sock suspenders). 'That's the way,' he said as he handed back the decoration. 'Now we must go and watch you on-stage – and correctly rigged!' It was probably the only time a real monarch has shown a stage one how to dress.

That was a happy day during the forties. But great sadness came after the end of the decade, for George VI, never physically robust and now weakened by war and cancer, died on 6 February 1952 at Sandringham House, his birthplace.

His passing, which left The Queen a widow at fifty-one, was so heavy a blow that at first many people feared that she would retire and be rarely seen. Suddenly her life, her constitutional position as Consort, her whole pattern of existence had been changed. Her daughter had become the new young Sovereign, Queen Elizabeth II – and now it was to her, at twenty-five, that Buckingham Palace and all royal homes, all the posts and protocol belonged. At once, then, the parent Queen gave to the new Elizabeth her whole loyalty and experienced support, never for a moment overshadowing her.

But when, in those early weeks of 1952, the widowed Queen Mother wrapped her grief within herself and disappeared from public sight, and when the news leaked out that she had gone to Scotland and had bought for herself the far-distant and then ruined Castle of Mey, it seemed as though she had elected to live a private life. In the event she was soon to return. Her nature – and the pull of the public's love for her – brought her back to public duty. What she said, and not for the first time, was, 'Work is the rent you pay for life.' So, although with no state position now, but bearing the new title of Queen Elizabeth The Queen Mother, she was soon 'in the picture' again, beginning her 'third life'.

Clarence House, adjoining St James's Palace in London, is The Queen Mother's principal home and headquarters; and Royal Lodge, in the south-eastern corner of Windsor Great Park, her weekend retreat. Then there is Birkhall, her house on the Balmoral estate. There (and at times at Sandringham, too) she is contentedly a countrywoman, touring stables and cottages, perhaps striding out in the cold and rain for a picnic, trailing clouds of courtiers and corgis. The resilient figure in old mackintosh and gumboots is just as much The Queen Mother as the London lady in feathered hats, three-string pearls and brightly floating dresses.

Whether in the north or south, this lady is no stay-at-home. She is active patron of over 300 organisations; her public duties and private benefactions are beyond cataloguing. She loves, and understands, music, the theatre and especially ballet, the visual arts, and the world of education. She is a very mobile lady and has for many years jumped in and out of helicopters on her United Kingdom engagements. She knows the Commonwealth countries at first hand – and jetted round the world even before her fast-moving son-in-law, Prince Philip.

For half a century she has been a leading figure of National Hunt racing, an owner with many winners to remember. She it was, who firmly established steeplechasing as a British sport. But what really interests her, I have to add, is not betting, not the money, but horses and horse breeding. Nevertheless, she is so 'hooked' on racing that she still likes to go to as many meetings as possible; and she has the bookmakers 'blower' telephone service in Clarence House so that, if she is at home, she can have immediate information on the day's runners, the odds and the state of the course. It was from the stewards' box at a racecourse, incidentally, that there originated one of the best examples of Her Majesty's forthright, unstuffy nature – a reminder that there is steel as well as smile in her personality. It concerns one of her sharpest private commands. Someone switched on the television set in the box just at the moment when the crowds at another sporting event were singing the National Anthem. As soon as she heard the sound, The Queen Mother swung round and said, 'Oh, do please turn it off.' When the order had been obeyed, she added, 'So embarrassing if one isn't there – like hearing the Lord's Prayer when playing canasta.'

Stories of the way she keeps *other people* as full of enjoyment as she is, crowd my own recall of hundreds of engagements on which I have watched her. She will not be bound by formal step-by-step schedule. At the opening of a big new commercial building in the City recently, she unexpectedly broke through the routine line of office bosses in the crowded lobby to go across and spend time in chatting to typists, messengers and lift-attendants who had been squashed into the back of the hall. It 'made the day' for those people.

On another excursion in London to carry out a programme which suggested a dreary inspection of a down-river building development, The Queen Mother stopped her car on the way back through Stepney and called, quite unscheduled, at a pub she remembered from the wartime days of the blitzed East End. To the astonishment of the people in the street, and the suddenly welcoming landlord, she breezed into the hostelry, declined proffered champagne in the private saloon, and had a glass of beer in the public bar.

The Queen Mother is always at home with her regiments. Here she visits the Sir John Moore Barracks at Winchester.

The press adore her. Cameramen know that, though she is not a 'show off', it's pretty certain that if they are assigned to a Queen Mum visit they will come back with a usable picture – possibly with help. There was the time, for instance, on royal visit day at a showground when a mongrel dog strayed into the guarded enclosure where Her Majesty was walking. Sure enough, bouquet in hand, she bent down to pat the intruder. The attendant photographers got splendid shots of that – all except one, whose camera shutter jammed. The Queen Mother heard the man's curse and, turning back especially to stroke the animal a second time, called an 'All right now?' to one rescued cameraman.

But the best incident of all in Fleet Street memories, was when an objectionable fussy little civic official was noticed by The Queen Mother in the act of shooing an accredited photographer off the red carpet in front of a Town Hall just when she was arriving. Turning from the Mayor, she called across to the officious character, 'Please don't do that. Mr Devon is an old friend of mine, and we both have a job to do.'

My experience of the Clarence House 'Camelot' suggests a very happy court, employer and employees working smoothly and unpretentiously together – but I do get the impression that one of the household's problems is getting the boss to slow down. When I have had the pleasure of an 'in-house' lunch, with Her Majesty in charge, the occasions have been delightful with the conversation, constantly sparked by The Queen Mother, unstrained and full of laughs. Sheer fun (but never an invitation to a risqué story).

I recall after one visit I boastfully displayed a bruise on one of my fingers which was the legacy of a corgi snap. I was rather sad when the dog-given 'royal badge' faded, for it showed that I had experience of the pets who are the innermost personal guards of the lady of the house. Remembering lunches at Her Majesty's home, there was one June day when our hostess, dressed for summer, elected to have a little lunch party in the garden rather than indoors, even though the weather had suddenly turned bleakly unseasonal, and I found myself shivering beneath windswept trees, and envying the lady-in-waiting who was wrapped in a woollen stole provided by her employer. The Queen Mother herself sat eating and laughing most happily, impervious to the east wind.

Her Majesty would be horrified, I believe, if anyone said to her that Britain had a 'television monarchy'; but the televising of state occasions – the broad sharing of purpose and pageantry – has always had The Queen Mother's support, and inevitably she is a featured figure of decades of outside broadcasts. But she has never, in the ordinary course of events, lent herself to performing especially to studio cameras. Thus, whilst her patronage of Royal Variety Performances through many years is legendary, it is not her way to join show business characters in chat-shows or indeed to air her personal

For half a century The Queen Mother has been a leading figure in National Hunt racing and what really interests her is horses and horse-breeding.

views publicly, however much her younger relatives may at times disport themselves. Perhaps she may not like all she sees on 'the box', but she does not interfere: she is the family's matriarch, not their controller.

Certainly she could not control the part played by all the members of the House of Windsor in the world acclaim for Her Majesty's ninetieth birthday, that milestone which was publicly marked by those celebrations that began months before the actual day, and by tidal waves of flowers and cards and gifts sweeping over Clarence House on 4 August. The year of 1990 had to be an unprecedented year. The lady of the house is Britain's oldest-ever Queen – but the special birthday salutes were much more than hurrahs to *longevity*.

How has she changed since I began to follow her career? I am often asked that question, and I have to answer: not at all. True, she herself might confess to feeling a little drained sometimes at the end of a full day's engagements. But nobody sees her tired. The point is that when you see her in her home, whenever she greets you with that effortless smile, those clear blue eyes and the lilting voice, notions of elderliness are not present at all. So through the years there really has been no change in behaviour and habit, style and spirit. The blithe nonagenarian admired by the world today has evidently never lost the inherent sparkle that was in Elizabeth Bowes-Lyon when the girl came dancing down from Scotland and shone like a sunbeam in a dark Palace over sixty-five years ago.

As to herself today, The Queen Mother is uninterested in the age business. Let others do the arithmetic, whilst she continues to enjoy the new mercies of each returning day.

INDEX

Page numbers in italics refer to illustrations

The Queen Mother celebrates her eighty-ninth birthday. This special birthday portrait was taken by Norman Parkinson at Castle Mey, one of her homes in Scotland.

PICTURE CREDITS